NEW 9 95

Jeremy Tyggr
.2909 SE
Lavei ST.
206-5776

D1616790

The Art of
GOALKEEPING

By the same Author

Bob Wilson's Soccer Focus

The Art of
GOALKEEPING

BOB WILSON

PELHAM BOOKS

LONDON

First published in Great Britain
under the title *Goalkeeping*
by Pelham Books Ltd
44 Bedford Square
London WC1B 3DU
November 1970

Second impression December 1971
Third impression June 1973
Fourth impression December 1976

First published in this second edition 1980

Copyright © Bob Wilson 1970 and 1980

All Rights Reserved. No part of this publication may
be reproduced, stored in a retrieval system, or trans-
mitted, in any form or by any means, electronic,
mechanical, photocopying, recording or otherwise,
without the prior permission of the Copyright owner.

Wilson, Bob
    The art of goalkeeping.
    1. Soccer – Goalkeeping
    I. Title
    796.33'426   GV943.9.G62

    ISBN 0 7207 1278 5

Typeset by Granada Graphics,
printed by Hollen Street Press, Slough
and bound by Dorstel Press, Harlow

Contents

Introduction

In this book I am attempting, for the third time, to unravel the art and mysteries of keeping goal. In 1963, whilst studying Physical Education at Loughborough College, I chose Goalkeeping as the subject for my thesis. It was based entirely on my school playing days and three years at college learning to be a teacher. I had also flirted briefly with the professional soccer world, being on associated schoolboy forms with Matt Busby's Manchester United when I was fifteen, and then as an eighteen-year-old amateur with Wolverhampton Wanderers at the time of Stan Cullis. Of course I thought I already knew it all, hence the thesis. With a bit of luck it may have been read by six people, but if nothing else it served its purpose in helping me to qualify as a schoolteacher.

My second attempt reached a far wider audience. It was in fact the forerunner of this book, and a complete update of those ideas from college days. Written in 1969 and entitled *Goalkeeping*, it now contained six years' professional experience at the Arsenal Football Club. Unfortunately almost five of those six years had been spent in the reserve side or third team, and whilst that late apprenticeship taught me a lot I didn't know previously, it wasn't exactly experience from the very top level. Still, the first twelve months as the club's number one goalkeeper had ended in a Wembley League Cup final appearance, and disastrous as it was – we lost to Swindon Town 3-1 in extra time – the moment seemed ripe to tell the world how to keep goal!

Of course, again I was being too presumptuous, but at a very crucial stage of my playing career the work served another useful purpose. It helped me formulate new ideas about the goalkeeping art, and the fact that my name went into print as a so-called authority did no harm to my confidence either.

So to *Goalkeeping* Mark III. Well, a great deal has happened in the years between my last effort and this one. After the League Cup disaster against Swindon there followed in successive years several Arsenal triumphs or near-triumphs. In 1970 the club won the European Fairs Cup, in 1971 the coveted League Championship and FA Cup double, in 1972 there was a losing appearance in the Centenary FA Cup final, and in 1973 we were runners up for the Championship. In all, and counting the 1969 League Cup final appearance, there were five glorious seasons of finishing first or second in a major competition.

Not only were they five exciting seasons, they were also invaluable for the experiences they provided; the good games, the bad, the high moments, the low, the glory and the despair. With all this new-found knowledge I could have rewritten the book there and then. I'm glad that I resisted the temptation because since those 'heady' days a calculated decision to retire from playing while still on top has led to a fresh challenge and a new career in broadcasting. More important for this book is the coaching of goalkeepers which I have been able to undertake in recent years, in particular with the professionals on the staff of my former club, Arsenal.

This regular coaching commitment has undoubtedly added greater weight to my arguments and theories on goalkeeping, and as a result I hope that this third book on the art proves useful as a guide, a comfort and perhaps even an inspiration to all aspiring custodians.

Bob Wilson

1

'You've got to be mad!'

The traditional theory that to be a good goalkeeper you need to be at the very least eccentric, at the worst totally mad, has never been proved one way or another. The truth is that many different types of individuals have become fine 'keepers but all have faced and experienced those moments of isolation which leave onlookers with no alternative but to form a conclusion that 'they're all stark raving bonkers' – moments when you are left exposed in one-against-one situations and moments when, without thought for life or limb, you decide to dive head-first into a forest of flying boots.

If as a 'keeper you thought about this kind of hazard for too long, I suppose you could drive yourself to distraction. But the art of keeping a bag of air out of the rigging is really a mixture of instinct and cool calculation, and as such I submit that the age-old lunacy theory is inaccurate – a myth. Having said that, the following experiences from my own goalkeeping career include plenty of evidence as to why the men who wear the number one jersey need to be 'a little different' from the rest of the team.

The beginning

It would be easy to state that all goalkeepers are born not made. If that were true 30 October 1941 was the most significant moment of my football career. However, there was another moment when my destiny seemed to be decided for me. It was Christmas 1949, the presents were all open, but only one commanded my full attention, a bright blue goalkeeping jersey given to me by one of my 'uncles' – Dr David Lees and his wife Anne. Blue had been chosen because Scotland played in that colour; David Lees was Scottish and so too were all my immediate family. An eight-year-old couldn't appreciate that the rules at the time stated you could only play for the country of your birth – in my case England. So the rest of that Christmas day was spent dreaming of the time I would walk out at Hampden Park. Little did I know that a mixture of hard work and fate would enable that dream to come true twenty-two years later.

The competitive spirit

I have no doubt that a good competitive spirit is again something with which you are born. Ultimate success, though, depends on many circumstances, not least of which is how inherent competitiveness is nurtured, and by whom.

My brother Hugh takes most of the credit – or is it the blame? – for my fierce and at times ungracious will to win. He was nearly three years older than myself and another naturally gifted sportsman who played football just as often as I did. The trouble was, being three years older he and his pals were always that much better, and stronger. I could not and would not accept the fact and competed with almost ferocious intensity to try and prove a point. It was right that the first face I should see at Wembley after Arsenal completed the 'double' in 1971 was Hugh's. My moment was his too.

Inspiration

I doubt if there has ever been any sportsman or sportswoman who has reached his or her own peak without help, guidance and inspiration of others. Family, friends, schoolteachers, coaches – all play a part. But the greatest inspiration generally comes as a result of hero worship, identifying with an individual who has already reached the top.

In my case it was a blond giant called Bert Trautmann, a German prisoner of war who was to break down all barriers of hatred with his goalkeeping for Manchester City. I'm not sure my father ever understood my choice. Having fought in the First World War and then lost his two eldest sons, my brothers Jock and Bill, who were shot down and killed while serving in the RAF in the Second World War, he was understandably reticent about Bert Trautmann. To me though, Trautmann was the inspiration I required to scale the heights. There was something extra special about the way he remained so alert, his commanding physical presence and above all the way he dived at people's feet. It was a save with which I was equally at home. Many times as a youngster I would close my eyes and see myself as Bert Trautmann and the fact that I was eventually able to emulate some of his achievements was as a direct result of the inspiration he provided.

The goalkeeping tightrope

It is often said that like good wine the better goalkeeper matures with age. That it is a fairly accurate assessment, but really it doesn't matter how old or how young you are, there will still be moments when the knowledge and training you have acquired counts for nothing. For one reason or another things go wrong. It might be a technical error, a rush of blood to the head resulting in a bad decision or even worse, something beyond your control. The game of football, never mind keeping goal, is full of highs and lows, and unless you come to terms with that fact you have little chance.

The problem is that those ups and downs can occur in the same game, and a true story involving one of the great goalkeepers of all time, Pat Jennings, serves to illustrate the point. It is a tale about Pat but in effect it is an experience all 'keepers have shared at one time or another.

The story goes like this. Pat was playing in a representative youth match for Ireland. On his own admission he was finding it difficult to maintain the real consistency he would have liked. In the first half of this game Pat had a nightmarish time. Three or four goals slipped by and he did little to inspire confidence within his team mates. The second half, though, was an entirely different story. Where he had lacked composure he now found confidence, punching, diving, catching and keeping his side from a drubbing. The glory of being between the sticks returned in full and despite losing the game, Pat left the field heartened by his second-half performance. From the depths of despair he had returned to a feeling of competence, even cockiness.

As he was just about to leave the field an elderly gentleman, clearly an expert on the game over the years, approached Pat and patting the Irishman on the back, remarked: 'Well done, son! You were absolutely great, and I'll tell you what, you were ten times better than the silly fool in goal in the first half!'

A backhanded compliment maybe, but a lovely example of the tightrope that goalkeepers tread.

Highs and lows, ups and downs

It is perhaps partly because of the isolation of the job, partly because disappointments far outweigh moments of pleasure, that 'keepers are considered a bit daft. And it's true that if you are unable as an individual to come to terms with the ups and downs you should consider playing in a different position or even take up another sport. I have no easy advice for the moments when things go wrong, other than to be honest with yourself. Look closely at your performance and learn from your mistakes, should there have been any.

As for moments of success, well, they are easier to deal with. Enjoy every second of the triumph for the rest of the day and possibly the next, but don't dwell on it. The old saying that you are 'only as good as your last game' is accurate, and that applies more to the goalkeeping position than any other. The whys and wherefores are unfolded in ensuing chapters, but here are a couple of examples from my own playing career that should help to keep you sober.

As I explained earlier, 1969 was my first full season in the Arsenal side. Respectability in the League, fourth place, and a League Cup final appearance against Swindon Town were a good start on paper. In reality that Wembley final against what was then a third division side was an experience that ended in sheer un-adulterated desperation. If possible it was even worse than that.

Try and imagine it. The mighty Arsenal humbled 3-1 by a third division team. It was all going to be so easy, and I even admit to imagining how it would feel on the lap of honour.

Several reasons for the disaster were put forward. Perhaps we underestimated Swindon a little. Then there was the inspired performance by my opposite number, Peter Downsborough, who thwarted numerous shots on target. Don Rogers' two-goal performance for the Wiltshire side was also important, plus the fact that only two of the Arsenal side had been able to train for ten days because of a 'flu epidemic. Wasn't the Wembley pitch a great leveller as well? The decision to have horse-jumping there had left a ploughed field which, with heavy rain, turned into a quagmire.

Excuses, excuses! The real truth of our defeat was that a mix-up between Ian Ure and myself presented Swindon with a gift goal in the first half and from that moment there was an element of desperation about everything Arsenal did, whilst Swindon made their own luck, and in extra time ran out worthy winners. The disappointment of losing was hard to cope with, but the sneers and jeers which accompanied our downfall made it much worse. In that situation you either capitulate, lose confidence completely and go into your shell or stick your chin out boldly and set about proving a few folk wrong.

I believe the Arsenal success over the next four years was born in the defeat at Wembley and the fact that the achievements came from the efforts of virtually the same players speaks volumes for the character of the squad. Certainly the Fairs Cup win against Anderlecht twelve months later provided the greatest scenes the fans have ever witnessed at Highbury. And of course, one year later, the return to Wembley was a sweet one. The League Championship had been won at Tottenham on the Monday evening and five days later on Saturday 8 May, Arsenal emulated the achievements of their North London neighbours ten years earlier by beating Liverpool 2-1 and adding the FA Cup to the League title.

Even that memorable day was not without its heart-stopping moments for the Arsenal goalkeeper. With no score after ninety minutes, the game went into extra time. A Liverpool attack built on the left. As Steve Heighway cut into the box with the ball, the 'keeper left his line anticipating a pull-back, only to be surprised by a shot between him and the near post.

For five minutes a season full of achievement and consistency, everything I had worked for, was lost. I was the man whom fate had singled out to cost Arsenal the double. Forget it. Get on with the game. There's still time. The thoughts that went racing through my mind at the time are as vivid now as when they occurred. All the record books show now is that Arsenal won the game with a classic goal from Charlie George, but believe me, for those five or six minutes after Heighway's goal I came as close as I had ever done to thinking that goalkeeping was a rotten pastime.

There are many other memories of that day in 1971 but one in particular has remained with me. The Liverpool 'keeper was a young man enjoying *his* first full season in the first team. His name, Ray Clemence. I was aware as we shook hands that he was close to tears. It's always difficult to produce the right words of consolation at such moments and mine at the time seemed inadequate – 'Don't worry, Ray, you'll be back. It's possibly my last chance. There's lots of time for you.'

Needless to say I have enjoyed watching Ray Clemence's career since then, and been delighted with the remarkable success he has achieved.

Fate, luck, hard work . . .

In this opening chapter I have touched upon aspects of goalkeeping which have all played a part in my own career. If I had to summarize the reasons for my eventual success, I would list burning ambition, hard work, a fair share of luck and finally fate. How do you explain fate? I'm not quite sure, other than to recall a couple of instances which on reflection just seemed destined to happen.

Like getting a taste of the Arsenal first team when the side was inconsistent, and breaking an arm in my second game. Whilst the team stuttered and spluttered and different players were tried and rejected, I faced a long road to recovery and by the time another chance came my way a side of rich promise was blossoming. Common sense suggests that had I avoided injury I might easily have been one of those youngsters who were rejected and put on the scrap heap.

Then there was the moment when that blue shirt of Scotland became not only a possibility but a reality. Why should the game's governing body decide to change the international rules in 1971 and permit players the choice of playing for either the country in which they were born or the country of their parents' birth? It was a controversial decision, but as far as my folks were concerned the fact that I was born in Derbyshire meant little or nothing. The whole family was a Scottish family, with Scottish blood, and the blue jersey presented to the eight-year-old football-crazy youngster for Christmas in 1949 signified the fact. Twenty-two years later a mixture of fate, luck, ambition and hard work earned me a second one!

2

What makes a 'keeper?
The personal qualities

Banks's positional play, Yashin's presence, Clemence's reading of the game, Shilton's reactions, Jennings's catching ability, Trautmann's courage . . . the aim of this chapter is to present a picture of the ideal goalkeeper both physically and mentally. However, before even attempting to list the recognized qualities needed to keep goal, I must stress that we are all different in physique and mentality. Of course there may be similarities between individuals in both aspects, but at the end of the day you have to polish qualities within your game that come naturally to you and work constantly on the areas you find difficult.

These can be mental problems, like difficulty in concentration, or physical ones, with say a weight problem or possibly a lack of inches in height. The player who is born perfect in all respects, an out-and-out natural, is a rarity, and that applies to many great international players over the years. Therefore the first essential ability for goalkeeping is perhaps a strange one.

The ability to look at yourself

No one can analyse an individual better than the individual himself. So throughout a goalkeeping career there should be a brutally honest assessment of physical and mental qualities, and of whether efforts to improve deficiencies are being successful. There must be similar honesty in assessing performance. Avoid excuses at all times, unless a deflection or the like has not been spotted by others and you are on the receiving end of unfair criticism. Constructive criticism never hurt anyone, and the day you don't need good advice or opinion, you will be lost.

16

Hopefully the chapters on technique and training will give you a guide when assessing your performance on the field, but first let's return to the personal qualities that are recognized as important for goalkeeping.

Height

I am certain there will be many youngsters who will have read up to this point reasonably happily, but who are now worried that they will be written off because they are not six feet tall and don't ever look like being so. The numerous letters I receive on the subject of height are worrying, because in effect the lad who writes has already built up a psychological fear that his lack of inches could be costly.

Well, let me immediately ease such fears by saying that there are many many examples of outstanding 'keepers who were not only under six feet but two or three inches below. As a youngster I would travel to Sheffield every weekend to watch alternately Ron Springett of Wednesday, who was five feet ten inches, and Alan Hodgkinson of United, who was five feet nine inches. Not only did both 'keepers play in the first division, but they also won England international caps – Hodgkinson five in all and Springett thirty-three.

Having used Alan and Ron to make a point about height, I am now going to be honest and say that in my opinion a six-foot-tall 'keeper has an immense advantage over the smaller man – as long, that is, as he possesses the necessary agility to go with it. For high cross balls especially, those extra inches make the task more simple. Similarly, one often sees a small 'keeper dive full-length and acrobatically turn a ball away, where a tall agile 'keeper would more often than not hang on to the shot and kill the move completely.

So my ideal 'keeper would be between six feet and six feet two inches, always assuming that he has the required agility and speed to go with it. As always there are outstanding exceptions, not only in smaller 'keepers but in taller ones. One of my closest goalkeeping friends is Joe Corrigan, a gentle giant who performed miracles for Manchester City and who, but for the brilliance and

consistency of Ray Clemence and Peter Shilton, would have won
more than the handful of England caps in his possession.

Joe is six feet four and a half inches tall, but in the early part of
his career it was of little advantage to him. That was because he
couldn't marry those additional inches with his physical bulk.
There always appeared to be a slight weight problem, and until he
had a long hard look at himself he remained the butt of the Maine
Road crowd's jeers. To his eternal credit, big Joe, always a glutton
for goalkeeping work, began to diet, and from that moment he
never looked back. The inconsistency in performance disap-
peared, he became a great favourite with the Maine Road crowd
and international honours followed. Joe's story provides a great
example of how a talented individual was honest with himself and
brought his weight into complete harmony with the distinct advantage he already had in height and reach. It also leads me nicely
to the next personal quality to be considered, that of weight.

Weight

Once again it is unwise to be specific about how much goalkeepers should weigh, but as you could see in the case of Joe
Corrigan it is closely related to height. The following list of British
'keepers in the late Seventies further illustrates the point:

'Keeper	Team	Height	Weight
Ray Clemence	Liverpool	5' 11½''	12st. 9 lb.
Peter Shilton	Nottingham Forest	6' 0''	12 st. 10 lb.
Joe Corrigan	Manchester City	6' 4½''	14 st. 8 lb.
Phil Parkes	West Ham	6' 2''	14 st. 5 lb.
Pat Jennings	Arsenal	6' 0''	13 st. 4 lb.
Paul Cooper	Ipswich	5' 9''	10 st. 10 lb.

In theory, the weightier the 'keeper, the more difficulty there is
likely to be with his agility, and in particular getting down to low
shots. Smaller men obviously have a lower centre of gravity and
tend to be excellent gymnasts. Against that, weight is useful in

one-against-one contact situations, like the high cross into the box, when goalkeepers often have to withstand some tremendous pounding. Then it's not just a matter of body weight but strength.

Before I move on to this subject, a word of encouragement to those who feel they have a weight problem. I'm sure it will gladden your hearts to know that Willie J. Foulke, affectionately known as Fatty Foulke, played in goal for England in 1897 and later appeared in three successive FA Cup finals with Sheffield United. Not too extraordinary in itself you might say, until you learn that the former Shropshire miner was six foot two inches tall and weighed twenty-two stone three pounds. That was at his peak, and in his last games for Bradford, before saving shots for a penny a go at a circus sideshow, he weighed 26 stone! Legend also has it that he was as light on his feet as a ballet dancer!

Strength

The importance of strength in a 'keeper's armoury is not restricted simply to contact situations and withstanding challenges. It is useful in throwing for distance, in kicking both a dead ball and a ball from the hands, and in helping to counteract the mud patches and heavy grounds that are part and parcel of British soccer. It is not easy to spring powerfully when there are two or three inches of mud around. To get airborne and achieve those vital inches, it's a question of using the strength built up by regular training sessions in similar conditions or periods of weight training.

I think it right to offer a warning that, as with so many aspects of goalkeeping, you must find the right balance when adding bulk and building strength. There was a time when England 'keeper Peter Shilton received much publicity for undertaking regular sessions on an army commando course. Frankly it was around that period of his career when I was of the opinion that he looked top-heavy, almost out of proportion between upper body and lower limbs. Peter may argue differently but I thought that for a while he went over the top in his desire for peak fitness and strength. As his career progressed there was a much better balance about his work.

Fitness

Later in the book I deal in more detail with a goalkeeper's fitness, but at this point, and having just dealt with weight and strength ratios, it is appropriate that I have my say about general fitness.

'Keepers are often the centre of discussions about fitness, but for the wrong reasons. 'He doesn't need to be as fit as the outfield player,' is the general cry. What a load of rubbish. In my experience, 'keepers are fitness fanatics, so much so that if you asked an outfield player to submit himself to a goalkeeper's training routines, he would exclaim: 'They really are mad!'

The point is that 'keepers need specific fitness based almost entirely on the type of work and movements they have to perform. In particular, suppleness, mobility and agility are vital and should be sharpened to a fine edge. If any coach feels this can be done in general squad training, he is badly mistaken. Certainly 'keepers should take part in general fitness activities, but not at the expense of specific work designed for his specialist role.

Concentration

Have you ever watched goalkeepers who, when the goal is not in immediate danger, spend time gazing around or, even worse, chatting to spectators? You can guarantee they will be the same 'keepers who regularly make silly, often costly, errors. Concentration for goalkeepers is all about coming off the field after a game where your team has won comfortably and in which you have had little or nothing to do, and climbing in the bath as shattered as the rest. I used to do that regularly in my days at Arsenal, and although at first the lads would laugh and ridicule my statement about being 'shattered', gradually they grew to understand that what I was referring to was not tiredness of body but tiredness of mind.

At the peak of our success, in 1970-71, we found that teams would come to Highbury with the sole intention of not conceding a goal and therefore guaranteeing at least a draw. Consequently as much as ninety per cent of the play took part in our opponent's half. For me, the lonely-looking figure at the other end, it would have been all too easy to look around, try and estimate the crowd, think about what I might do after the game, or whatever. Had I done so it would have been fatal.

I estimate that in any reasonably matched game, and regardless of how much one side may get on top, the 'keeper at the other end will be called into serious action a minimum of six to eight times. So concentration at all times is imperative, and to maintain it I practised a golden rule. I think it could work for you, as well.

Follow play to every corner of the field, regardless of distance from your goal, and imagine that when the opposition win possession they can shoot and score past you. In effect, you are facing a team of bionic men who have the power to fire a shot in accurately from a hundred yards or more. By believing this to be a possibility you not only concentrate like mad but find yourself constantly adjusting position and narrowing the angle. The same rule applies when you play away from home, but generally you find concentration easier, as the opposition have more of the play and tend to be on the attack much more frequently.

Concentrating for ninety minutes is like watching a good movie of the same duration. It is such a short time really to forget all other activities and become totally absorbed in the job at hand. Never forget that one brief relaxation can spell defeat for your side.

Confidence

A goalkeeper who lacks confidence in his own ability to keep the ball out of the net should not be a goalkeeper, whereas a 'keeper who always looks the part will instil confidence throughout the team. It's as simple as that.

You communicate confidence by displaying safe handling, making good decisions and by shouting instructions and encouragement. There is, however, shouting and shouting. If your defence has let you down and you save the day with a brilliant stop, it is stupid and irresponsible to immediately be seen to give them a 'rollicking'. Unfortunately too often top-class 'keepers do just that. They are angry and can't control their feelings in the heat of the moment. What they should really be doing is encouraging, not knocking. Defenders know only too well when they've made an error. Then is the time to lift them. After all, you are the last line of defence, and when all barriers are down it's your job to prevent a goal.

We are all human, all make errors and at times need to be encouraged. In the goalkeeping position you are better placed than anyone to give a little shout when someone has done something well. 'Well done, John,' 'Brilliant, John,' 'Hey come on, you can do it, John,' and so on. Out-and-out 'rollicking' serves no purpose whatsoever unless you are sure a team mate is hiding and trying to make excuses for himself, and that's not often the case.

Nor is it likely that you, the 'keeper, will ever start a game brimming with confidence. Such is the tightrope goalkeepers walk that you can never guarantee that it's not going to be one of those days when you tip a ball onto the post and it still goes in, rather than those beautiful moments when you seem to do precisely the same thing, only it comes back to you off the woodwork. Therefore the early touch is quite crucial and the longer you have to wait for it the more your confidence can be drained.

There's little or nothing you can do other than put on an ACT, and I mean just that. Butterflies affect ninety-nine percent of all sportsmen and women, but woe betide you if you show it to your opponent. Games can be won or lost before a ball is kicked or a gun fired. One of my best friends was John Cooper, who so tragically lost his life in the DC 10 crash near Paris some years after winning two silver medals for Great Britain in the Tokyo Olympics of 1964.

I'll never forget 'Coop', as we called him, telling me about the warm-up preliminaries to his 400 metres hurdles final. In his own mind he had eliminated five of his opponents on past events and current form. At the same time, he felt he was not going to be quite good enough to win the gold medal from the American Cawley. It was therefore a matter of silver or bronze between him and an Italian athlete. As they eyed each other during warm-up, Coop never betrayed his inner fears. Suddenly the Italian turned to him and said in broken English: 'Cooper, you strong'. John without batting an eyelid replied: 'Yes, I know'. In that brief moment the race for the silver medal had taken a definite turn in favour of the Englishman.

So you see what I mean by acting. Go out and at least look the part and when that first save is called for, trust in yourself and your ability.

Hands

Ultimately your ability as a goalkeeper is judged by the way you use the most important part of your equipment – the hands. I say hands, but in effect I must also link them with wrists and fore-arms, because all need to be equally strong in order to withstand shots of often awesome ferocity. Apart from being the most important part of your armoury, the hands indicate the 'keeper's specialist position.

Is it important to have large hands? It's a question often asked, but one can only theorize and state that it must be advantageous to possess a large pair of hands. One of the great 'keepers of all time, Frank Swift of Manchester City and England, had a huge hand measuring 11¾ inches from his little finger to the tip of his thumb. And goodness only knows what span another great international, Pat Jennings of Northern Ireland, possessed! Pat's hands resembled a couple of shovels, and an example of how he used these God-given attributes to good advantage is the way in which he could seemingly catch high crosses one-handed. In fact the real truth of that particular save is that if Pat had made an error of judgement on the cross, rather than palming the ball away like me or, I suspect, you, he still had a hand large enough to hang on to the ball.

Ultimately, though, it is not how *large* but how safe hands are, and a huge part of a goalkeeper's confidence stems from the ability to handle well.

Agility

Undoubtedly one of the more important aspects of goalkeeping is the ability to throw the body into a variety of positions at speed. This is basically an instinctive action, but the natural agility you are born with can be sharpened by constant training and practice.

The author demonstrates the agility so necessary to a successful 'keeper.
Photo: Photopress.

If there is any fear whatsoever of hurting yourself on landing, then don't take up goalkeeping. In the job, you have to be capable of lifting your body off the ground and hurling it at varying speeds and angles towards the ball before landing in an often untidy and sometimes even painful heap.

I have already mentioned that smaller, slimmer individuals are, in theory, able to dive around more naturally than the bigger men. As always, though, it's a case of swings and roundabouts, and apart from advantages in reach which the taller 'keeper possesses, constant practice and training can leave both body types with no glaring differences or weaknesses.

Mobility

Some people would consider that mobility is the same as agility, but although they are very closely allied they are nevertheless different. One may often observe a 'keeper showing remarkable agility but not consider whether he could have avoided the spectacular by using his feet. A fault of all too many 'keepers is that they lack mobility, yet have agility. Some even do it on purpose to be 'flash', but that's a dangerous game, and to be a good goalkeeper the two attributes of agility and mobility must be present.

Footwork and speed off the mark is mobility as far as the 'keeper is concerned. Once a decision is made to go for the ball, getting there and the time it takes are all-important. The crucial factor, though, is whether a 'keeper sees the attempt at goal and goes for it immediately from where he is, or whether he manages to get in a couple of movements with the feet, which invariably allows him greater reach and, as important, eradicates the spectacular. Safe is far better than spectacular. The greatest British goalkeepers ever seen – Swift, Hibbs, Banks, Clemence, Shilton etc. – have all based their game on good mobility allied to equally sound agility.

Positional sense and anticipation

All the 'keepers just referred to would tell you that you never stop learning when you are between the sticks. Experience is something even the best coach cannot teach. He can relate his own goalkeeping experiences, but only by finding yourself regularly in new situations will you be able to cut down shooting possibilities. It is depth of experience which improves what should be a basic instinct for positioning yourself in the correct place and anticipating what is about to happen.

In fact anticipation means being one step ahead of the opposition. I have found that it also helps to put yourself in the other man's shoes when danger threatens. You can do this by experiencing what it is like to be confronted by a goal guarded only by a 'keeper. Small-sided games or practice matches are good enough to give you the 'feel', so insist that you occasionally play out of goal. By so doing you will get an important insight into an attacker's mind. For example, think of yourself as a forward bearing down on goal, who is faced by the 'keeper, but who is also supported by a team mate. The decision that has to be made is whether to dribble round the 'keeper, or just draw him forward before passing into the path of the supporting player. If the 'keeper is doing his job properly and presenting a formidable barrier, the odds are that the pass to the side will be the choice.

Now come back to goalkeeping, where you're facing just that situation. You should be able to anticipate and read the mind of the man in possession. He may prove you wrong occasionally but experience will give you the edge in anticipation. Having said that, you must always credit opponents with as much intelligence as you have yourself.

Clearly positional sense and anticipation are closely allied. Positional sense is essential in that the 'keeper must at all times know where he stands in relation to his goal. In theory it is illegal to mark your six-yard line, but in practice it is an impossible rule for referees to implement unless as a keeper you are silly enough to scar the pitch in full view of him. Referees and linesmen don't have eyes in the back of their heads, and if you desperately need a marking to help your positioning there is little or no way they can spot where 'mysterious lines' come from. I know I stand to be accused of encouraging ungentlemanly behaviour, but as far as I'm concerned as long as you don't break a line marking you are not breaking the rules as written. Even if you have a guilty conscience about this matter there is always the penalty spot from which to take bearings or the flags on the halfway line. You certainly need some object or marking at times when you become disorientated.

I've said how closely allied positional sense and anticipation are, but let me warn you that although generally they work together, there are also times when the partnership can lead you into trouble. My great hero Bert Trautmann eventually won an FA Cup medal when Manchester City beat Birmingham 3-1 in the 1956 final. A year previously, however, he had been on the losing side when, despite making many fine saves against Newcastle, he also got caught out with a goal scored by Bobby Mitchell. Trautmann was at his near post with Mitchell almost on the goal-line. The 'keeper's position was good but his anticipation suddenly betrayed him. Assuming Mitchell was at too tight an angle to score, Trautmann started to move to his left as the winger drew his foot back, hoping and expecting that the ball would be pulled back into the goalmouth. The 'keeper's movement was made a fraction too soon and when Mitchell shot for the near post, Trautmann was hopelessly beaten. City eventually lost 3-1.

I have always considered it a supreme irony that the goal Steve Heighway scored for Liverpool against me in the 1971 Cup final should be very similar – cutting in from the left, seeing me make a move to anticipate a cross and firing the ball in off the near post. Fortunately for Arsenal and especially their 'keeper, the mistake didn't prove to be fatal!

(The ability to *narrow the angle*, although vitally important in keeping goal, is nevertheless more of an acquired technique than a personal quality and as such I will deal with it in depth in Chapter 4.)

Courage

I have always got myself into deep water when talking about courage because like many other football coaches I am of the opinion that regardless of natural talent or ability, you have not got a cat in hell's chance of a successful career without the personal quality of courage. As you will see, the importance of this quality does not purely apply to 'keepers. It is just as essential for the outfield player as well.

What must be understood is that there are two types of courage and I'll begin with the one most regularly applied to goalkeepers.

Instinctive courage usually refers to the ability to dive fearlessly at an opponent's feet, and only if you have experienced the sensation of a huge forward bearing down on goal can you realize the difficulty some people have in doing just that. But like everything else it must become instinctive. The person who thinks twice before going down is generally injured. This is not to say that a 'keeper doesn't get injured by an instinctive dive – he does. But on the majority of occasions a 'keeper who dives at feet will escape un-

Courage is essential in a 'keeper, and it is displayed here by the author who, coming out to clear the ball, gets a boot in the chest (Arsenal *v.* Ajax, European Cup, 1972). *Photo: Syndication International.*

scathed while saving a certain goal. That fact alone makes the action justified, whatever anyone else says.

I consider that my goalkeeping career started in earnest when I was fifteen and continued until I was thirty-four. In that time, it would be impossible to even hazard a guess at the amount of vital saves made at the feet of opponents. Admittedly it was a save which came more naturally to me than any other, but at the end of the day its importance far outweighed the torn left ear, eight broken ribs, one broken arm and even a punctured lung which I sustained, not to mention countless stitches in my head.

Of equal importance to raw courage – and I mean equal – is *thinking courage*. It may not be familiar terminology, but 'thinking courage' means the ability to make decisions boldly and bravely while knowing that you could easily be proved wrong. This particularly applies to balls crossed close to the six-yard box, when it is all too easy to hide, stay on the goal-line, and hope that one of your defenders gets to the ball before an opponent.

If you are scared to make decisions you will fail for sure, but by being confident, bold and adventurous you will be rewarded in the long term. Once again you are gambling to a degree, but with increased experience the gamble becomes a highly calculated one with an ever-improving success rate in terms of saves.

So the courage of your convictions and instinctive courage are both absolutely crucial, and especially if you are thinking of a career in the game. I can only stress their importance by saying that they represent the difference between being a top-class or an average player.

Personality

Contrary to popular belief you don't necessarily need to be of an extrovert nature to be a good 'keeper. In fact I would go as far as to say that the majority of top goalkeepers are quiet, sensitive individuals off the field of play.

The great Manchester City and England goalkeeper Frank Swift had an altogether larger-than-life personality which matched his extraordinary physical appearance. At the peak of his career he was able to joke before a game, and by doing so reduced the nerves of his colleagues to a bearable minimum. No doubt they were unable to assess just how nervous their big 'keeper was himself. It was, of course, an *act* on Frank's part, one built up over the years of playing at the top level and begun in dramatic style in 1934. In that year Frank Swift played for City in the FA Cup final when they met Portsmouth. He was just nineteen. As the final whistle signalled a 2-1 victory for City, the youngster fainted in the Wembley goalmouth. Nervous tension and strain had taken their toll.

Pat Jennings's personality was totally different from Swift's. You would struggle to recall many occasions when he could be seen waving his arms or yelling at team mates. Only once in fact do I remember him showing any inner feelings during a game, and that was when he saved two penalties in the course of a match against Liverpool at Anfield. Even then it was a case of upraised clenched fists and a smile of satisfaction that flickered very briefly.

Against that there is the Sepp Maier type of 'keeper. The former

West German international was a complete extrovert in dress, manner and physical appearance – long shorts down to his knees, gloves that appeared suitable for wicketkeeping in cricket, very distinctive mannerisms and hair styles that varied almost as frequently as the weather.

Gordon Banks was another who never worried that his joking before England international games would backfire on him. His personality remained outgoing but calm, before, during and after the most severe of tests.

As for myself, I preferred to go into my own little world in preparation for a game but without losing touch with what I considered essential duties. After satisfying myself with a warm-up routine, I would venture around the dressing room and have a word with every player; 'Good luck, Ray,' 'Come on, Charlie, show 'em what you can do,' 'Keep shouting, Frank,' and so on.

As you can see, four professional goalkeepers with four basically different personalities. At the end of the day, whether you are noisy or quiet does not really matter. The important thing is to be consistent in your relations with the rest of the team. Moodiness will almost certainly cause edginess and needless worry in those around you.

So there you have it – the ability to look at yourself, using your height, weight and strength to advantage, a safe pair of hands, sound fitness, good concentration, confidence, agility, mobility, a good positional sense, anticipation, courage and personality – fourteen qualities which are important if you have ambitions to keep goal and are hoping to achieve consistency.

Consistency – the supreme aim

However good a goalkeeper you become, you will always make errors ranging from those of a positional nature right through to the inexplicable. I am not going to offer any ambiguous advice. You must be positive. Real consistency is measured in terms of error. The 'keeper who makes fewest errors over a period of time will always be superior to one who can be brilliant and make seemingly impossible saves, but who regularly costs his team the game with lapses of concentration.

The greater the heights scaled the more responsibility you feel. So much is expected of you, but you alone fully understand the fallibility of a goalkeeper's role.

Don't ever complain. You would not want it any other way. A hero's role is what you have chosen, so go out and fill it in such a way that when errors inevitably occur, you have the fan who watches you play regularly remarking: 'My goodness me, that was unusual!'

3

Importance to the team

'Don't be silly. It's obvious. A goalkeeper's importance to a team is simply whether he can keep the ball out of the net or not!' That's the usual reply to the question about a 'keeper's importance, but it's not altogether true.

The one position on the field where good ball control is of only minimal importance is goalkeeper, where you may be a hero one day and a mug the next. The uprights and crossbar of the soccer goal enclose an area of one hundred and ninety-two square feet. It may not seem very much if you happen to be a forward bearing down on goal with the ball at your feet, but when you are the lad in sweater, cap and gloves, given the unenviable job of keeping the ball out, that yawning space can seem as big as Wembley Stadium.

Glamour role or not, 'keepers are made to pay for the privilege of their position, and unlike those who play in outfield positions, their mistakes can be costly, often crucial. Soccer is a game of split-second decisions. Forwards make them, so too do defenders and midfield men, but on nobody do they descend as suddenly and frequently as on the 'keeper. Catch or punch? Go or stay? Questions like this are with him all the time. In certain situations there are quite clear guidelines and obvious principles to follow. Often it's a case of only one option being open. At other moments there is a choice which must be made bravely for right or wrong.

In a way it's one reason why it is difficult, even dangerous, to be too emphatic about goalkeeping. Much of it is simply instinct and common sense. Laying down hard-and-fast rules is dangerous, because as often as not, you never know quite what is going to happen until it is actually happening. The goalkeeper's importance to a team can be broken down into three categories, only one of which directly involves shot stopping.

32

Importance as a defender

Ultimately the 'keeper's role in defence is the most important because when everything else has failed and all defensive barriers are penetrated, he alone can stop a goal being scored.

The impression created by a 'keeper has a direct bearing on the confidence of any side. If the 'keeper is seemingly impregnable, especially in the early stages of a game, it has a considerable psychological effect on the rest of the team. His actions can instil or ruin confidence.

'I'll never forget a quote I heard as a youngster from Vincente Feola, the coach of Brazil's 1958 World Cup-winning team. Brazil had beaten the host nation, Sweden, 5-2 in the final, with the young Pele scoring twice. All questions had been directed towards the brilliant attacking qualities of the Brazil team. Feola delayed praising his attackers, in order to say: 'What you forget is the save our goalkeeper Gilmar made when the score was 1-1. It was just as vital as the goals we scored at the other end. Unfortunately few people yet realize that a brilliant save by a goalkeeper is every bit as important as a scoring shot. The 'keeper is seldom the subject of back-slapping.'

Of course times have changed. No longer could Feola's quote be applied quite as strongly. 'Keepers are appreciated in the modern game and they take as much credit for a team's success as the star goalscorer. Where time has tended to stand still is in the appreciation of a goalkeeper's wider role within a team, one which embraces not only being the last line of defence, but also the instigator of attacks, a director, tactician and general observer.

Importance as an observer

As the rearguard of a team and restricted to a penalty area, the 'keeper is perfectly placed to observe his ten colleagues in their play, both individually and as a unit. In fact a 'keeper is in a position to observe all twenty-one other players on the field of play. From his isolated position he is able to consider whether his defence is covering correctly, and whether problems posed by the opposition can be easily solved. Even with a defence which operates a simple diagonal covering system, it is within the 'keeper's job to instruct and if necessary correct when things go slightly wrong.

I've already mentioned the different ways of shouting, and in my playing career I found a warning call to one of the Arsenal back four often helped consolidate things. Similarly if the defence was having a bad time and being split open, I was better placed than anyone else in the team to spot where the trouble had originated.

Advice, encouragement, warning calls and occasional out-and-out 'rollickings' are all important and make up an integral part of the team system and confidence. When it's half time or even after the game is over a 'keeper must never be afraid to have his say, to the rest of the team, to the coach or to the manager.

Importance as a director and tactician

Preventing goals may be the major objective when keeping goal, but there is great importance attached to what is done with the ball once saved.

Whenever possible an attacking movement should be attempted with every clearance. An aimless throw or kick is not only a waste of an opening but it is likely to increase the goalkeeper's own work. Invariably a hasty, thoughtless clearance comes straight back, and if the defence has been under pressure there is no chance for it to regain its composure. I must admit it took me quite a while to appreciate the usefulness of taking my time in certain situations. The full range of throws, kicks and clearances at one's disposal should be used only when appropriate. If you are having a lot of success with a long punt, then use it until its usefulness falls away, and likewise if short throws to defenders are not working but causing trouble then cut them out.

On some days a goalkeeper can exploit weather conditions. A difficult sun in a defender's eyes is one thing to look for; a strong wind in your favour another. Determine which is likely to cause the most danger and capitalize on it. Above and beyond these tactical areas a goalkeeper should be prepared to marshal his defence at all times. It is not a lone responsibility, however, and all team members should be prepared to make helpful calls. The only area over which a 'keeper should have complete dictatorial control is the six-yard box. It is his territory, and although he can't ban intruders he can show who is boss. This applies at all set pieces, which are covered later.

In concluding this chapter on the goalkeeper's importance it should be stressed that although ultimate perfection in the position is the aim, everyone has faults. Therefore recognition of one's faults and weaknesses becomes important so that priorities can be singled out. The greatest priority of all, though, is to keep that bladder of air out of the rigging by any means at one's disposal.

4

Techniques — accepted and acceptable

It has taken a long time, far too long in fact, for the importance of the goalkeeper to be recognized. However, better late than never. Almost all games have 'turning points', those crucial seconds when a game can be won or lost. Invariably they involve the man between the sticks, who either saves the day with a great stop or has a disaster in the form of a shocking error.

Unfortunately, 'keepers themselves can never be absolutely certain of the outcome of any incident in which they may be involved, but by a mixture of good technique and awareness of other possibilities they need never be afraid. In this chapter I will endeavour to list the recognized techniques essential for goalkeeping, outline any inherent problems in each of them, and hopefully suggest ways of improvising.

The last statement about improvising will surprise only those people who have never experienced playing in goal and therefore are unable to appreciate fully the strange happenings that arise. By 'strange' happenings I mean deflections, balls swerving and dipping, and so on. At such times all the good intentions and accepted sound techniques count for little. Instinct, razor-sharp reflexes and well-practised awareness alone can save the day, and however ungainly one may look, as long as the ball stays out of the net the method of saving is totally acceptable. So before we get under way with all the recognized techniques, be quite clear that all types of save involve an *accepted* method, and an equally *acceptable* yet very unorthodox method.

This chapter on goalkeeping technique falls into three parts:
Catching and shot stopping;
Distribution;
Set pieces.

Catching and shot stopping

Basic position for keeping goal

A goalkeeper is required to dive, reach, jump, sprint, back-pedal, move sideways and make a variety of other movements, at less than a second's notice. In order to do so he must find a starting position with which he is completely comfortable, confident and relaxed. Whenever I've seen film of lions or leopards waiting to pounce on some poor unsuspecting prey, I've been struck by the stillness of the animal and the perfect balance. Well, there are similarities for the goalkeeper.

Imagine the ball is the prey. The best chance you have of pouncing on it and stopping it is if there is a completely controlled and balanced starting position. In this respect, the 'keeper's basic position should be with feet slightly apart and knees slightly bent. The main part of his weight should be on the soles of his feet with the immediate spring coming from the toes. The body is inclined forward slightly, but beware bending too much otherwise you could get caught with a lob or chip. As always we tread the tightrope between right and wrong. It really is as thin as a rope as well, with the difference between success and failure a matter of fractions of inches and seconds.

Anyway, the body is bent slightly forward and so too are the *arms* – but here again you alone must 'feel' a comfortable position, the one that is right for you. If you incline your arms, and consequently your hands, very low you should appreciate that shoulder-high or head-high shots require a greater movement than a midway position. Similarly a high arm and hand position demands awareness of the extra movement involved for a low ground shot. Ideally therefore I would advocate a midway position, one assuring equal confidence and success with low or high shots. Although the hands are the most important part of the 'keeper's armoury, it is *footwork* which generally makes saves.

Here again you must find your own ideal. I was a bouncy, alert type of 'keeper, and by that I mean one who needed to feel full of spring all the time. It took me a long time to appreciate that my basic starting position, being so bouncy, had really a dangerous edge to it. Not when the ball was out wide or thirty yards or more from goal. You can afford to be as springy as you like then. But the closer the ball comes to goal the more the 'bouncy' type 'keeper must beware and start to lower his spring so that contact with the ground is hardly lost at all. Shots can and do occur when a keeper is on the upward bounce, and if that spring is too high you will be in trouble trying to get down to the low shot.

By keeping in contact with the ground when opponents are in and around the eighteen-yard box you give yourself a good chance of being able to move the body instantly for whatever is demanded. What emphasizes the 'tightrope' we walk is the reverse situation where a 'keeper is 'dead' on his feet, seemingly lacking in any alertness or spring whatsoever.

Watch the top professionals and you will see a wide variety of basic positions, but rest assured that the 'over-alert' 'keeper knows of the dangers his style holds and that the 'less alert' player has ways of coping with his particular method.

It should go without saying that any basic position in goal-keeping involves keeping an eye on the ball at all times and even when play is at the other end. A reminder of the points made earlier about concentration: follow play constantly, move around the box angling at all times and, whatever the distance, remember the 'bionic man' opponent who can score from eighty, ninety or a hundred yards. If you do, your concentration will never waver and your angling will also benefit.

Getting the body behind the ball

Think of the body simply as a *barrier* and you are on the way to reliable goalkeeping. Think of goalkeeping in terms of being able to stop shots by hands alone and you are a million light years away from filling the role even adequately.

Of course the hands are the most vital part, because by using them well you can 'kill' shots and often inspire confidence in colleagues. Even greater confidence, however, is instilled by the 'keeper who looks unbeatable. That involves not just handling ability, but the ability to form a complete human barrier capable of

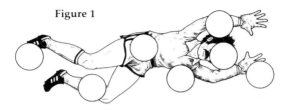

Figure 1

saves by head, shoulders, chest, stomach, arms, legs, knees, ankles and feet. Only the hands are able to hold the ball consistently, but the rest of the body should provide a barrier capable of equal inspiration. See Figure 1.

I don't intend to list intricate techniques of saving by toe, shoulder and the rest of the more unorthodox areas, but just don't underestimate their value. So many saves are instinctive and spontaneous, and as long as your mind is alert to the wide variety of possibilities, with the body trained to react instinctively, you will get away with murder.

The basis of all these less conventional saves comes from solid technique in more predictable areas.

Catching a ball

The difference between the right way and wrong way to hold a ball is again small. All that is essential is that there is little or no chance of it slipping out of the hands once caught. So the best way of ensuring safety is to form a cradle shape with the hands. This suggests they are quite close together when contact with the ball is made, and so they should be. A barrier formed by fingers and palms is priority number one, but if the hands are too far apart there is a strong possibility that the ball could slip straight through.

It doesn't matter whether the ball is coming towards you on the ground, at chest height or above your head, the shape and distance between both hands and fingers should remain the same. In all but saves well above or to the side of you, remember the insurance of getting some part of the body behind the ball. There should be a conscious effort at all times to present strong fingers, wrists and forearms. For a ball struck with force you also need plenty of flexed muscle to absorb the pace.

Once contact is made, 'kill' the ball by pulling it in close to your body. The more you perfect this and make it one smooth movement, the more chance you have of taking the pace out of a shot while it is still effectively in flight.

IMPORTANCE OF HEAD WHEN CATCHING AND SAVING

As you can appreciate by now, all parts of the body are important when catching and saving. Few, though, are as crucial as the *head*. The realization, acceptance and reaction to any situation starts in the head, but that's not the point I'm stressing here. What I mean is that sharp movements with the head are a direct cause of fumbled shots and even delayed reactions.

Think about it for a moment. A boxer is taught to bob, weave and duck in the course of defending himself, but the movements of the head are always controlled sufficiently for the eyes to pick up the opponent's jabs and uppercuts. It is exactly the same when keeping goal. Not that I would advocate bobbing, weaving and ducking your head all the time. On the contrary you should always aim to keep that part of your body as controlled as possible. But the excitement and danger created around goal is such that you are continually adjusting your position, and sharp movements caused by a pass can lead you to move the head too quickly. At this instant your vision has to become less sharp, even blurred.

It's easy to test yourself and find the amount of head movement you can cope with. Start by gently moving your head from side to side, and gradually increase the speed and distance of the movement until you are shaking your head fairly violently. Somewhere in the middle of those extremes is a control limit suitable for you.

IMPORTANCE OF FOOTWORK WHEN CATCHING AND SAVING

You may feel it's taking a long time for me to get around to the techniques required for the best-known saves, but everything I am telling you now about basic position, basic handling and use of the head is vital to all types of save. So it is with footwork.

Except when you are called on to sprint from goal for the ball played over the top of the defence or on high crosses, the majority of saves involve a foot movement between as little as half a yard and as much as two or three yards. Gordon Banks's memorable save from Pele in the 1970 World Cup, which I describe in detail later in the book, was as much about footwork as anything else. Not six yards of footwork but half that amount, and chopped strides at that.

The 'keeper who saves in spectacular style when he could have made it look comfortable is a bad 'keeper. Good footwork cuts down the margin of error and improves positional play.

Gathering low balls and back passes

You may choose one of two methods of collecting the ball that comes in low: either you get down on one knee or you bend down with both legs in line behind the ball and knees slightly bent. Before enlarging on them, I want to stress that you must never lose sight of the importance of providing a stopping surface for the ball apart from your hands. Even the simplest of back passes can land you in trouble. If you assume that it is going to be a 'doddle' – an easy save – you are asking for trouble. I have knelt down to receive numerous back passes, and on several occasions been saved by shoulder or even face when the ball has struck a divot or hit a slippery patch.

The best example I know of a low 'easy-looking' shot finishing up in the back of the net was Cardiff's 1927 Cup-winner when Arsenal's Welsh 'keeper, Dan Lewis (no, it wasn't me!), allowed a simple shot from Hugh Ferguson to slip through his hands. That goal has been attributed to Lewis's brand-new jersey, which was supposed to have been shiny, having never been washed. It's a good yarn but nonsense. Dan Lewis let in the goal because his concentration lapsed momentarily and certainly long enough for his basic technique to be found wanting.

Nothing has changed much since poor Dan Lewis's time. Goalkeepers are still being proved 'mugs' and I suspect they always

Two ways of gathering low balls. *Photos: John Child.*

will be. Either of the following methods of collecting low shots (see above) would have saved Dan Lewis his embarrassment.

1. With the body directly in line with the oncoming ball, and legs kept almost together, bend down and place the hands palm-upwards and behind the ball, scooping it up towards the chest immediately contact is made. Some 'keepers prefer to bend the legs a little, while others like to keep the legs almost straight. I believe the first position is more compact and better should the 'keeper need to move away quickly.

2. An even safer method of gathering the low ball is to kneel on one leg with the body slightly turned. The normal safety rules are applicable and the advantage is a slightly bigger barrier presented.

Catching a chest-high ball

The chest-high save should quickly become a most comfortable and confident one. You have nearly everything going for you.

Nice height of shot, plenty of barrier and very little movement of the feet. You can make it an easy stop if you allow the ball to meet the chest, curl both arms underneath it and then allow the body to move backwards slightly in order to cushion the pace. You will make life difficult for yourself only if you lose concentration, assume it's easy or are too tense. If the body is rigid, with no give in it, the ball could strike it and fly away before you can curl fingers around it. The greater the pace of the shot, the more you must 'ride' the catch, and move backwards.

As with the low shots there is an alternative method of catching. In this, one hand is placed above the ball and one below it with the elbows kept close to the body. Arguments for this method claim that it is safer and the ball is less likely to bounce away from the chest. Only experience will tell you whether either or both are suitable for you. I must admit to using both on occasions, but I did find the second method – the over-and-under one – an unnatural movement.

Catching a waist-high ball

This is the easiest of saves, despite the fact that the actual shot is generally a powerful one. All that is necessary is to break the force of the ball by taking it with cradled hands and guiding it to the stomach. The hands are palm-upwards and once the ball is met you should engulf it between the forearms and the chest.

The ball can be taken by the hands with the elbows slightly in front of the body or tucked into the side of the lower chest with the elbows at the side and the hand wrapping over the ball. The force of shot should already be assessed before catching and any real pace taken out of it by a movement backwards.

The only problems you are likely to face will be self-inflicted.

Diving for shots to the side

Diving is quite the most spectacular element in the goalkeeping art. It is claimed that it wasn't even part of a 'keeper's armoury

until the turn of the twentieth century when a Southampton cus-
todian, B. Robinson, dived to his left to save in a game his club
played in Vienna. If the story is true we can safely suggest that Mr
Robinson revolutionized the goalkeeper's technique from that
moment with one fell swoop!

Anyway, diving for shots demands great elasticity and not a
little courage from goalkeepers, but when successful the rewards
for them are enormous. Diving for shots to the side can be divided
into shots:

a) which are able to be covered by the body;
b) which are saved at full stretch and held;
c) which are parried.

So much applies to both types of diving save –(a) and (b) – that it is
best to outline the *common factors* first.

It is good footwork which usually enables a 'keeper to dive and
still get his body behind the ball. If he doesn't use his feet he may
well still save the shot, but only in spectacular fashion at full
length. The same can't be done for shot (b).

The ability to throw the body into a variety of positions at
speed – that's how I defined goalkeeping agility in Chapter 2,
and here is one of the saves where it comes into play. There can be
no hesitation, no fear, otherwise it will be too late. If a shot to the
side is hit from a distance of more than ten yards, you ought to be

The author executes
diving saves to the
left (below) and to
the right (opposite).
Photos: Central Press.

able to get in at least half a yard's movement with the feet before diving. The further away the shot, the greater the time to move the feet and the closer the shot, the more pure instinct comes into play.

To young goalkeepers, diving represents some fear of hurting themselves on impact with the ground. They should be assured that if they throw themselves wholeheartedly after a ball they will never get hurt badly. A few grazes occasionally maybe, but a ball held safely with no resulting goal eradicates any pain.

Differences between the diving saves start to occur when it comes to holding on to the ball.

a) In the diving save which can be covered by some part of the body, the same principles apply as when catching a ball to the chest, but the major difference is that the impact with the ground on landing can easily dislodge the ball. To prevent this happening requires much practice in catching and diving. The key to success is to be compact on landing. As soon as the catch is accomplished there should be a concertina effect in the body, the ball being tightly held to the chest while the knees are drawn up as tight as possible.

As long as you hang on to the ball it doesn't matter too much which parts of the body take the impact, but as we are dealing with accepted and acceptable ways of doing things, I would say the ideal landing should be on outer arm, thigh and the side of the leg.

b) When the ball is out of reach of the body but just within reach of the hands the 'keeper should still attempt to catch if possible. If you are able to dive and catch but still get some bend of the arm you should still have little difficulty holding on to the ball, but the more you are at the maximum stretch, with arms fully extended, the more difficult the save. It is often claimed that a tall 'keeper is more easily beaten by a low shot, and it's true that shots close to the body always cause greater difficulty. But when it's a diving save to left or right, reach is far more important and a distinct advantage.

For all types of diving save, a strong fast take-off is needed, with knees slightly flexed. It is simply an extension of the basic position – the pouncing of the cat, remember?

c) The last resort in diving to shots, left or right, is the parry. It is completely acceptable to parry if all else fails or the pace of shots is such that you can't hold them. You always run the risk of the loose ball being seized upon and tucked away, but as the first priority in goalkeeping is always to give yourself a second chance, it matters little as long as the initial shot hasn't found the target.

Instinct, practice and game experience will sharpen your reading of any diving save, but for both the parry of the powerful shot and the deflection at full stretch there is an additional requirement of the hands, wrists and forearms. Each must be that fraction stronger and provide greater resistance to pressure than normal.

Diving at a forward's feet

Courage and fearlessness are key requirements of a goalkeeper, but in no area do they apply more than when a 'keeper has to dive at an oncoming forward's feet. It is a high-risk situation and one

where there is no place for cowardice. More often than not the odds are stacked heavily against the 'keeper when this type of save is called for. It epitomizes the role of the man who has the ultimate defensive responsibility in a team.

It would be irresponsible of me to suggest that diving at feet doesn't occasionally cause serious damage. My idol, Bert Trautmann, broke his neck in this manner during the 1956 Cup final, and Celtic 'keeper John Thomson actually lost his life by plunging at the feet of a Rangers forward during an Auld Firm game in September 1931.

During my goalkeeping career, diving at forward's feet cost me over twenty stitches around the head, a torn ear, several broken ribs, a punctured lung and a broken arm. What did I gain in return? Literally countless saves of the utmost importance, each one of which bolstered the confidence of the team and ultimately helped in the winning of a trophy or two.

The collision that broke a 'keeper's neck: Bert Trautmann (Manchester City) dives at the feet of Birmingham City's Peter Murphy in the 1956 FA Cup final. *Photo: Press Association.*

Liverpool's Ray
Clemence makes a
diving save at the
feet of Everton's
Mike Lyons. *Photo:
Syndication
International.*

I was never taught how to perfect the save, but simply watched
and absorbed Bert Trautmann's technique and found that I could
reproduce it instantly. Only occasionally does this happen, but if
you are as fortunate as me with any aspect of your own goalkeeping, not simply diving at feet, for goodness sake recognize the
importance of it at once. Anything that comes totally naturally is a
diamond which you should work at polishing just as hard as all
the less natural areas of your game. By polishing you could find a
save eventually sparkles so brightly that it becomes associated
with you and sets you apart from the pack.

Fearsome or not, diving at feet is an essential part of keeping
goal and I firmly believe that if done quickly and correctly the
likelihood of injury is very slight.

There are two methods of diving at or in front of an oncoming
forward, *head-first* and *side-on*. The whys and wherefores of both
cause much argument, but really it's again a case of what comes
naturally in any given situation.

HEAD-FIRST

By head-first we mean diving forwards with the hands and arms
obviously leading and the top of the head exposed. The fact that it
is the top of the head causes worry and has led to the argument

that it is far more dangerous than a sideways dive at feet. I dispute this totally and would start my defence of the head-on save by saying that out of the list of injuries sustained in my playing career referred to earlier, the majority of serious ones, i.e. punctured lung, broken ribs and torn ear, all occurred when I dived at feet side-on.

Think about it for a moment. The top of the head is a relatively small area, but the area represented by chest and full face is quite extensive. One represents a small area to be whacked, the other a sizeable one.

Really there's a lot of fuss about nothing, because in many instances the argument counts for nothing. Instances when in a packed goalmouth the ball breaks loose in front of you for a fraction of a second, or when a forward, clean through, loses control for a similar period of time. In either case you plunge instinctively, not with the brain telling you to go one way or another. Instinct is all-important, for a slight hesitation could result in a goal or injury.

Whether it be a one-against-one situation or a loose ball in a packed area, the technique is straightforward.

1.   Keep the feet in contact with the ground. If you bounce too much on toes at this time, you could be caught on an upward spring when the ball is momentarily 'free'.

2.   The 'free' moment of the ball is when it comes within your range either by a lucky bounce or when an opponent has lost control.

3.   When this occurs, act swiftly with the feet and the rest of the body.

4.   Try to be *balanced at all times* so that you can spring in a variety of directions.

5.   Attack with speed, power and strength.

6.   Reach for the ball with both hands, which must be as strong as ever.

7.   As soon as the hands make contact with the ball you can start to tuck, bringing the body from a long position into as small a ball as possible.

8.   Your momentum will carry you way beyond the point of first contact, so stay strong and be prepared for knocks to head, shoulders and arms.

One final tip when diving head-on at feet in a one-against-one situation. I want you to put yourself in the opponent's shoes. He's clean through but he's under pressure. Running with the ball and beating you has to be done quickly. Very few players can keep the ball under tight control all the time when running at speed. Somewhere on the way to goal there will almost certainly be a slight hesitation or miscontrol. That's the moment you're looking for. Spot it quickly and seize the opportunity with both hands. The opponent won't know what has hit him, so clearly it's a question of *timing*.

SIDE-ON

If the situation is one where the ball is 'free' for only a fraction of a second and you choose to dive side-on, I guarantee you will be beaten eight times out of ten. The side-on dive at feet must be undertaken when either everything is in your favour and you are clearly going to get there first or – the complete opposite – when there is no moment of miscontrol and the opponent has all going for him.

If you hold the advantage use your feet, act swiftly with a similar attack to the 'head-on' technique and get down on the ball before it's kicked. You might even be able to continue what is essentially a twisting movement and present your shoulders as a defensive barrier. Whatever the circumstances, grasp the ball firmly and draw it as quickly as possible into the chest.

When an opponent holds the advantage you dive with similar technique but your aim now is to *block*. The body is simply a

THIS PAGE AND OPPOSITE The author shows how to block at a forward's feet. *Photos: Syndication International and Sport & General.*

barrier and it's up to you to present as large a target as humanly possible. You are playing the odds and hoping that the shot hits you anywhere – head, chest, stomach, legs, knees, arms, hands or feet. It matters not. All that matters is that the ball stays out of the goal.

Remember, when you block but fail to hold, you have to continue playing regardless of a bit of pain. You also need equally alert defenders who can clear the loose ball and finish the job you started.

OUTWITTING THE OPPONENT

Apart from looking for a possible moment of bad control, you may be able, with experience and practice, to outwit an opponent who is running at you with the ball. When approaching him out of goal, you need to keep your nerve, stay upright and present a big target. Then at any moment you feel is right *throw a dummy* — a false gesture or movement one way which looks as if you have

committed yourself, although in fact you remain balanced and
ready to spring, more than likely, the other way.

The exaggerated movement can be made by dropping the head
and shoulder or simply one arm. When a player is running with
the ball, he concentrates on it exclusively, but his peripheral
vision, i.e. the outer edge or corner of the eye, will still pick up
your movements and may cause him to at least change his mind or
do exactly as you wish.

Now, a final *warning* which applies whenever you leave your goal
unattended. *Beware of the lob or chip!*

If your timing is badly out and you make your approach from goal
too fast or too obvious, there is every possibility that an opponent
will chip you. In the 1970 World Cup Brazil's Pele was in the
defensive half of the field with the ball at his feet when he spotted
the Czech goalkeeper, Viktor, standing near the edge of the penalty
area, eighteen yards from the goal. The long-distance chip shot Pele
attempted failed by no more than a yard, with the startled Viktor
left floundering in no-man's land. I have no easy tips for you in this
respect; experience alone will teach right from wrong, and even
then you might get caught out. So don't be afraid to fail. Instincts
invariably provide the correct decision.

Narrowing the angle

Without really meaning to, we have already touched on the area
which is considered by many to be the most essential one of all in
goalkeeping – narrowing the angle; the ability to place yourself in
a position which leaves an opponent with as small a target to shoot
at as possible.

Narrowing the angle is a mixture of common sense and applied
science. The 'keeper who stands in the middle of his goal and on
the line is going to need a miracle in order to save a well-struck
shot from sixteen to twenty yards which is aimed just inside a
post. A dive of some three or four yards would be required to save
the day. The 'keeper who had moved five or six yards off his line,
however, has at most a yard or two to dive for a similarly struck
shot.

These two examples illustrate both the meaning and importance of narrowing the angle, but they provide only a simplified explanation, and the more you consider this technique the more complicated it becomes.

For a start, shots rain in on goal from varying angles and distances, so the goalkeeper has to be constantly adjusting. The types of shot are just as variable. They can be low, high, chipped, swerved, bent, blasted. Time and practice prepare you for any eventuality, each of which must be recognized, assessed and acted upon almost instantly.

The main point to remember is that the closer to goal the shot, the more you must narrow the angle. With this relatively close-range save there is far less time to move your feet, whereas for distance shots from twenty yards and more there is time, however hard the strike, to get in at least a yard of movement with the feet. In this instance it is advisable to be little more than two or three yards off the goal-line, otherwise there is a possibility of being caught by a 'dipper' over your head.

Having sounded a warning on the wide variety of shots and the distances from which they are struck, it's time to outline the real theory of angling. I make no apologies for occasionally repeating myself, but the technique of narrowing the angle is crucial and you must understand it totally.

If you imagine that the goal-line between the posts is the permanent base of a triangle, then the changing vertex of this triangle is the position of the forward who is about to shoot. The goalkeeper must place himself as in Figures 2 and 3 so that his arms can almost touch both sides of the triangle. If the ball passes outside the sides of the triangle it will almost certainly miss the goal.

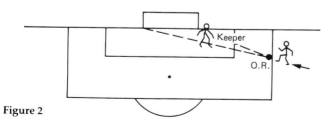

Figure 2

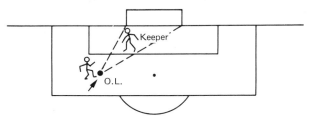

Figure 3

In Figure 2 the job is considerably easier, although the 'keeper has to guard against the possibility that the opponent with the ball might do the sensible thing and centre.

In Figure 3 the attacker has more of a shooting angle. The 'keeper cannot cover the area entirely, for if he is drawn too far out there is a danger of being 'lobbed'. By advancing a little, though, he can make the uncovered area of the goal seem very small. This is the whole object of angling, so it is far better to be bold and to take a calculated risk. Rarely will your decision betray you.

When the ball is directly in front of goal (Figure 4), even more of a risk must be taken. Then it's a case of cat and mouse, with the 'keeper advancing a little way and checking to see how the opponent reacts. If a shot isn't immediately forthcoming it's possible to move even closer. Of course in a game there isn't the same time that there appears to be when you are sitting writing or reading about this situation. Generally, when a breakaway occurs leaving a one-versus-one situation, the sole hope of saving a goal is to advance briskly and force the issue. Give the opponent with the ball too much time and he will pick his spot. By coming out of goal

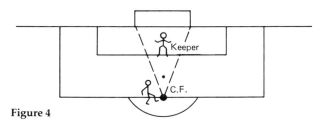

Figure 4

you make the forward reconsider his alternatives of whether to try and dribble around you or shoot.

If a 'keeper can cause any hesitation whatsoever on the attacker's part, he has been partly successful. It might even result in a brave plunge at feet to save or give defenders the chance to recover.

TURNING THEORY INTO PRACTICE

However brilliant one's knowledge of angles, it is of little use in practical terms without applying the following techniques:
1.   Very good footwork, which needs to be in the form of small, mincing steps. Alert and on the toes, but not too high.
2.   Small steps keep you in contact with the ground almost continually. Remember the point about bouncing too high on toes? It's easy to get caught on the upward movement.
3.   Apart from keeping contact with the ground, maintain a low upright body position. By this I mean a low centre of gravity, a comfortable basic position from which you can move fast in any required direction.
4.   Try and make yourself as big as possible, an 'incredible hulk', and physically intimidate your opponent by your size.
Anyone narrowing the angle has to be bold and courageous as well as trusting in his *instinct* to go or stay. Think positively and always be prepared to incorporate the art of *anticipation* when narrowing the angle.

Mind-reading and reading the game

Now we have an understanding of the value of leaving the goal-line to narrow the angle, we must go one stage further and appreciate why it is often necessary to take a calculated gamble to leave the goal completely unattended or to take a chance to dive 'early'.

'ABANDONING SHIP'

The earliest goalkeeping simply involved standing on the goal-line and stopping the ball from going in the net. Slowly but surely 'keepers began to venture off the line and began trying to dominate the whole of the penalty area. Nowadays the job involves even more than that, and apart from being *shot-stopper* and *box-bosser*, goalkeepers have become 'super-sweepers'.

How to explain it best? Well, most observers of the 1974 World Cup finals in West Germany would agree that there were two outstanding teams – the hosts and eventual winners, West Germany, and the runners-up, Holland.

In the Dutch goal was Jan Jongbloed, who with no disrespect looked to be one of the most ungainly men ever to pull on the number one jersey. Frankly he seemed to be constructed of spare parts, but although his goalkeeping caused some amusement because it was so unorthodox, in one area it was foolproof. Jongbloed's sorties out of the penalty area saved the adventurous Dutch on numerous occasions. Several times each game he would anticipate the ball played through, above or beyond his defenders and rush away from his charge to kill the danger.

Ray Clemence, the Liverpool and England 'keeper, was another vastly skilled at the art of reading the game and 'abandoning ship'.

Clearly *anticipation* is the key to success, and the essentials required to complete the save are as follows:

1.   Courage of thought and action – making a decision and sticking to it;
2.   Speed of thought and action – reading the problem instantly and acting upon it with similar speed;
3.   Good footwork;
4.   Composure when nearing the ball.

(*Remember*, if the 'keeper is moving quickly, as he almost certainly will be, caution is needed at the moment of contact with the ball. Rush the kick and there is every possibility that it will either be missed completely or sliced.)

Clearly this kind of save is closely related to those involving a calculated gamble. It is crucial that goalkeepers familiarize themselves with all types of situation, learn to read the mind and thoughts of attackers, and get to know how the forwards tend to react under pressure.

ANTICIPATION

Let me give two simple examples of anticipation by a 'keeper within the penalty area.

1) A forward cuts in at an angle to goal. Because it is at an angle obviously there is less of the goal to shoot at, and rather than blast hopefully the forward will be looking to try a chip or, even more likely, to pass to a colleague. Here the 'keeper holds a slight advantage and should be able to anticipate the possibilities.

2) If a winger has the ball at his feet and is wide on a flank, the inexperienced 'keeper is likely to immediately rush to the near post, just in case there is a shot at goal. Experience, however, soon tells him that if the winger is really wide, there is no chance of a goalscoring attempt from that distance. Instead a cross should be anticipated, and the 'keeper should edge off his line a yard or two and find a position from which he can attack any type of cross – near post, middle or goalmouth, or far post. The closer opponents come to goal the more difficult anticipation becomes.

Making an error of judgement when reading a through ball or a cross from the flank need not be fatal. There is room for recovery. Make a similar error when opponents are close to goal and there is little or no hope. The ball will be in the back of the net before any recovery is possible. Advice isn't easy regarding *close-range* anticipation. What I would say is:

1.   Don't be scared to fail;
2.   Trust your instinct;
3.   Gamble sensibly, calling upon your experience and knowledge of the way forwards react.

If there is any time available to you when facing attackers, the aim should be to put them in some sort of a quandary. The more problems a forward faces the more likely there is to be a *change of mind*.

A final word on anticipation and the ability to read the game. The two are virtually inseparable. Both require a *knowledge* and *experience* of shooting possibilities, of opponents, of general movement and direction of play. Relative comfort in both areas will only come when a goalkeeper finds himself in situations he's been in before.

The high ball — to catch, to punch or to deflect?

By now you should be very familiar or very bored with my constant reference to the *goalkeeping tightrope*. Perhaps it's a little of both! Well, steel yourself for a further dose of tightrope-walking because we are about to debate what is arguably the most difficult 'trick' of all – how to deal with the high cross. The degree of difficulty is such that I would compare it to the circus tightrope performer doing a forward somersault blindfolded and without a safety net.

No other area of goalkeeping receives as much leg-pulling or joke-telling as the high ball.

'Our keeper is so bad at high crosses we call him Daffodil! He only comes out once a year!'

'Our 'keeper is like Dracula – hates high crosses!'

These two standing jokes about the goalkeeper's problems on the high ball serve to underline that this is one of the most difficult of saves. It is also recognized as such by outfield players, managers and coaches. Consequently tactics are developed to exploit any goalkeeping weakness there may be.

It is the save which sorts out the men from the boys all right, but it is a technique perfected down the years by British 'keepers in particular. In fact the main reason British 'keepers command so much respect on the world scene is their confidence and consistency in dealing with the high ball.

Why all the fuss?

Isn't catching the ball at its highest point a simple matter of keeping the arms at full stretch and watching the ball? The answer is 'yes', *but* – there are a few other considerations as well. Like the type of high ball, which could be any one of the following: near post; far post; mid-goal; under the bar; swinging away; swerving in; dipping; curling; hit with pace; mishit; up and under; struck from the touchline, goal-line, edge of the box, centre circle, etc. And that's not all! There is also the possibility of the penalty area being packed with as many as sixteen or eighteen players, especially at free kicks, when big defenders on the opposing side move up to add their height to that of the forwards.

What to concentrate on first
The first thing I would suggest is that you retrace your steps, turn back a few pages and go over the section on anticipation and reading the game. Both are required if you are to achieve a high level of success with the high ball.

Then what? Understand that quick *decision-making* is vital – a decision to 1) catch; 2) punch; 3) deflect.

CATCHING

No one needs to be told that catching is by far the best of the three alternatives. The effect of a catch on the goalkeeper is to instil enormous confidence, but not half as much as it does in the rest of the team. The 'keeper's complete command of the box lifts team morale quicker that any other element. Defenders feel that their

Catching a high ball.
Photo: Central Press.

own responsibility is reduced considerably, especially when the opposition includes a player renowned for his heading ability.

There is a completely opposite effect if a goalkeeper stays on his line, hides, shelves his responsibility and relies on reflex saves. Defenders are unnerved and the 'keeper's indecision is conveyed like an epidemic to the whole team.

Catching method – without challenge and under pressure
If you are wondering why there should be any differences at all between collecting high balls unchallenged and those under pressure you would be absolutely right. There is none. The balance, positioning and timing are identical and so too is the determination to make the ball yours. The reason I mention the two separately is simply to make you aware that nothing is easy where a high cross is involved. 'Keepers often go to gather thinking they are alone, but no one has eyes in the back of their head, and a late challenge from behind surprises the man who is overconfident or too relaxed.

Once again experience and practice help with the decision when and when not to go, but there is a golden rule! The *six-yard box* is the 'keeper's domain; a kingdom which must be ruled completely. All centres, corners, free kicks and long balls within this area should be his responsibility.

Responsibility doesn't end there either. Depending on where the ball is kicked from and how much pace it has on it, anywhere up to and even occasionally beyond the penalty spot can also be 'bossed' by a goalkeeper.

Position of 'keeper in relation to crosses
When a ball is struck from a wide flank position, somewhere near the touchline, the keeper can be central or backward of the central part of the goal. He has *time* on his side and even a sudden driven ball at the goal itself should be easily within his grasp as long as he is alert. The basic position, though, enables a 'keeper to move in all directions and to all types of cross into the goalmouth – near, middle or far.

Danger signs occur the *closer* to goal the ball is brought by an opponent before being crossed. If the 'keeper remains central or even backward of centre he will be quickly exposed at the near post either for direct shots on target or for crosses. So as an opponent creeps in field with the ball, the 'keeper must move towards the near post and at times even past it. A classic example is Gordon Banks's save from Pele which is outlined in detail in Chapter 5.

It is important that an understanding of one's starting position and the need to boss the six-yard box should precede the actual *technique of taking crosses*, which we will delve into now.

1.   Goalkeepers should always face the direction from which the ball is coming. It is personal preference alone as to whether the starting position of the body is square-on to the cross or side-on. On contact it must be square-on, but I for one found that a flat starting position with my head turned in the direction of the ball was the most comfortable. My theory was that I could attack in any direction with almost equal speed. Facing square-on, although having a fractional edge on forward movement, was highly vulnerable to deep back-post crosses or even middle-of-the-box balls. The important thing is that it was right for me. I felt happy, comfortable and confident. Most important of all there was a high consistency and success rate when I ventured to catch. If in doubt, experiment during training or practice games until you gain similar confidence.

2.   'Keep your eye on the ball' is a rule that applies to every ball game, but in no phase of a game does it apply with more urgent force than that of the goalkeeper going out to catch a high ball. The temptations to take the eye off the ball are great. Obstacles in the shape of well-meaning defenders or hostile attackers are generally littered everywhere. 'Keepers must not ignore them but neither must they fear them. A healthy respectful awareness is the answer. Friend or foe, they have to be overcome, even if it costs all parties a knock or two!

3.   *Strength* is therefore an essential. It is required on take-off, and when bodies collide. If a 'keeper is unprepared for a body blow, he will automatically drop the ball. In fact even when he's strong and positive a challenge might still be enough to dislodge the ball.

4.   Wherever possible, and incidentally it is not always possible, a *call* should be employed. 'My ball, Jack,' or 'Leave it to me, Jack,' and so on are sufficient communication once players get to know

A

B

A sequence of photographs showing the author catching a high cross –
and hanging on to the ball despite taking a battering.
Photos: Express Syndication.

C

D

each other. The call should be made as early as possible and delivered with authority and confidence. If time is available, defenders will get out of the way. When a cross is suddenly lashed in with pace, calling is an impossibility. Every fraction of a second is required for effort of movement. Instinct and reflex action come into play.

5.   Movement towards the cross should be smooth and timed to perfection. Hesitation or jerkiness can be fatal.

6.   So *judgement* of the *distance* and *flight* of the ball must be precise.

7.   It helps before *take-off* to be in a coiled-spring position. Good, sharp, quick movement with the feet puts the 'keeper into a position to gather himself before springing.

8.   *Lift-off* requires power and strength from the legs. I say *legs*, but I really mean *leg*, because height is best obtained from a one-footed take-off, like a high-jumper. There are distinct similarities in the approach to lift-off for both types of athlete.

9.   A lot of the hard work has now been done, but there remains the all-important area of 'killing the cross' by catching cleanly. As with the take-off element, the ball itself must now be attacked, with collection occurring at maximum height.

10.   Achieve maximum height and there can be no argument, when collisions occur, about opponents outjumping 'keepers to head the ball. The jump of both may be similar but the goalkeeper's advantage of outstretched arms and hands is far too great for any outfield player.

11.   After watching the ball right into the hands, elbows should bend to allow the ball to be brought swiftly down within the protection of the body and, if possible, clutched tight to the chest. The longer the ball is left exposed, the greater the possibility of it being jarred out of a 'keeper's possession.

12.   From the moment good contact with the ball is made, the whole body of the 'keeper should become compact whilst retaining its resistance to challenge.

The twelve-point plan just outlined for goalkeeping technique of the high ball assumes a great deal, not least of which is the *courage* required to leave the line.

In the chapter on personal qualities I finished the section on courage by saying that having it or not having it means the

The author saves a high cross under pressure. *Photo: Central Press*.

difference between being a top-quality player and an average player. Related to the goalkeeper and the high cross it means either playing a part boldly in defensive play and venturing into areas of difficulty, or 'hiding' on the goal-line and putting one's faith in the hands of others.

Trying to play safe has no part in this save either, simply because there is no safe area within it. It's a do-or-die situation. Go halfhearted for a cross and you'll be bowled over. Wait for the ball to drop until it can be clasped to the chest, and it will never get there. Instead it's more likely to be resting in the back of the net, headed there fractionally before it reaches the 'keeper's grasp.

So courage and the ability to gamble must be integrated with the basic techniques of going for the high ball. But *confidence* is of paramount importance. Once a 'keeper commits himself he must go all the way for it.

The opposition's view

Opponents will be attempting to make life as uncomfortable as possible. First they may try and outjump the goalkeeper in an attempt to *head* the ball. For this to occur, the 'keeper will have to make an error of judgement.

Then comes the type of challenge aimed simply at *impeding* — jumping into and at the 'keeper as he leaps to save. Nothing can be assumed, and although the majority of referees will spot such antics and award a foul, there are occasions when play goes on.

Finally there is the *distracting* leap. This is when an attacker moves directly in line with the 'keeper and the cross, but jumps far too early. The aim is to cause doubt in the 'keeper's mind, to pull him forward and underneath the cross so that he finishes flapping at the ball or missing it altogether.

Useful tips

The majority of tips already outlined for the high ball assume fairly predictable situations. I would hate to lull you into a false sense of security and therefore consider it essential to refer briefly to other aspects which frequently occur.

Trajectory of ball on cross   Because crosses are hit in a wide variety of ways (i.e. driven, chipped, hanging, swerving) it is dangerous to suggest that movement to all crosses is the same.

Believe me it isn't, but generally one of two ways will be adequate.

1. Crosses hit with pace, including those swerving away, are in one respect easier than those when the ball is in the air a long time. Crosses with pace require an early decision which is followed by almost instantaneous action. You are on your way before any doubts can creep in.

2. Crosses that hang in the air and take a long time to arrive can be far more difficult, a real nightmare. A 'keeper knows he has to go but timing of the attack is more complex. Go too early and there could be trouble. Jostling will be the greatest danger, bodily contact with opponents which prevents a good lift-off to catch. So when the ball takes time to reach, stay cool and *arrive late*. The timing of the 'keeper's attack should be such that an opponent is already anticipating that he will get the cross. Suddenly he needs to get the shock of his life as the 'keeper arrives late, but strong and positive, and prepared to take the catch at a difficult body angle.

Body angles   When there are bodies in the way the 'keeper must be prepared to collect the cross at a variety of strange angles, all requiring suppleness from the waist upwards. A variety of twists and curls are all essential and all the textbook stuff about solid upright positions means little or nothing. Improvisation takes over, all of it totally acceptable. See Figure 5.

Catching the high cross when moving backwards

Suppleness is also important when 'keepers are called upon to back-pedal to take a high cross. The twisting and bending of the trunk is in reverse. It *looks* at times to be a back-breaking movement, but the strength in the upper part of the body should be such that there is no problem. See Figure 6.

Figure 5   **Figure 6**

Here are three other points to note when catching whilst travelling backwards.
1.   The footwork has to be in the form of little mincing steps. Big
strides backwards will hinder rather than help. Short sharp footwork is all-important to cover the distances required.
2.   It is impossible to see who is behind you when moving backwards, so there is an additional need to be strong in case you run
into an opponent.
3.   When the actual catch takes place the 'keeper is likely to be
off-balance. The easiest and safest thing to do is to 'go to ground'.
In other words, as soon as the ball it held, the 'keeper should get
into as tight a body position as possible, and as soon as contact
with the ground occurs, the legs should buckle and the 'keeper
should roll. See Figure 7.

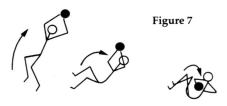

Figure 7

Protection
If you are a fairly experienced 'keeper already I feel confident you
will be with me on this section. If you are a beginner read it
carefully, because the protection I refer to is really an involuntary
movement of knee or feet. It is a controversial area because any
obviously bent knee or raised foot will lead to accusations against
goalkeepers of dangerous play.
    If a 'keeper coming out of goal *deliberately* straightens the leg
and points the toe after catching (see Figure 8), he deserves to be
booked. I have seen it occur, but very rarely. Putting the knee or
foot up is not even a special technique that can be practised. It is
simply an involuntary movement which occurs with any jump off
the ground where a ball is to be caught.
    Still photos have often looked horrendous, with 'keepers on an
upward or downward movement being caught in a pose that

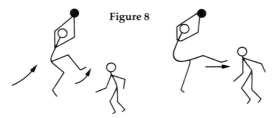

Figure 8

suggests they are intent on kicking an opponent around the head. If those who accuse (and they include spectators, managers, opponents and referees) had ever played in goal it would be no news to them that when you actually leap to catch you are totally oblivious to anything but the desire to catch the ball. Where knees and feet end up doesn't even enter a 'keeper's thoughts.

I'll never forget Roger Hunt, the former England and Liverpool striker, losing his head completely after I had caught a ball lobbed high into the box. My studs caught Roger in the chest as I came down but I wasn't aware that he was even close to me.

The argument about *foot-up* is one, perhaps the only one, in which I would plead for greater understanding by referees. A deliberate movement of intent with the boot should always be punished. But any experienced 'keeper will confirm my words that ninety-nine per cent of 'foot-up' incidents are completely unintentional.

Now it's time to move on to the two other alternatives a 'keeper faces with the high ball – punching and deflecting.

PUNCHING

Punching the high ball clearly comes a bad second to catching. It can look spectacular, but unlike a catch of any kind it does not *end* the attack. Punching is a last resort but none the less a very important requirement. It occurs or should only occur in situations of difficulty, and especially where several bodies hinder or block the 'keeper's route to the ball.

High balls of all types lead to collision courses, but experience will gradually help the goalkeeper to select the best action on

whether to catch or punch. Good punching requires:
1.   An early decision. Hesitate and all will be lost.
2.   Decisive movement.
3.   Concentration on the flight of the ball at all times. Forget that other players even exist.
4.   Solid contact with one or two fists.
5.   Distance – at least enough to avoid an immediate scramble and preferably eighteen to twenty yards.
6.   Direction – where and when possible towards the wings.

Single-fisted or double-fisted?

No hard-and-fast rules can be laid down. The degree of difficulty involved at any given time is the deciding factor. If there is time and the problems are reasonable, aim to punch *two-fisted*. The main advantage it has over the single-fisted punch is that two closed fists present a bigger striking area than one. One disadvantage is that with both arms upraised, the body is less protected.

For the *single-fist* punch it's vice versa. The free arm and hand affords some protection but one small fist permits only a small degree of error, and bad timing will see the ball missed altogether.

Technique   The approach and take-off is the same as for catching high balls, but when punching, a strong bent arm is required. If the arms are extended all the time, power to punch is reduced almost completely. Where two fists are used, they should be close together with curled thumbs and curled first fingers touching.

The vital aspect for both the double- and single-fisted punch is the distance covered by the fists and the speed with which they travel.

Distance   Rarely more than six to eight inches. A huge swing, and timing is likely to go astray with power also lost. Think of a knockout punch in boxing. Uppercuts travel a matter of inches. It's the same in goalkeeping.

Speed The knockout punch is also delivered fast, and here again goalkeepers share a similar need. So in effect we are talking about a short sharp punch, which at all times must be controlled.

As punching is a last resort, a means of overcoming what often seems a multitude of bodies, the 'keeper is hoping for a good clearance, one which allows both defenders and himself at least to

Double-fisted punch (left) and single-fisted punch (below). *Photo below: Provincial Press Agency.*

reorganize. The greater the difficulty there is in punching cleanly the more a 'keeper tries to simply buy time. Punching for *height, distance* and *width* all provide necessary seconds for the 'keeper to get himself balanced and well positioned should he face a follow-up shot.

Finally I would suggest that punching demands courage and aggression. There is no room for politeness or complaint. You must make your own luck.

DEFLECTING

There are two distinct and different types of deflection save. One is even more of a last resort than punching. A 'keeper is caught up in a pack of bodies and restricted in all-round movement. Frankly he is struggling to even make contact, but an open palm which turns on contact with the ball will often be enough. At least it sees the 'keeper attacking the heart of the trouble, but because the ball

Deflecting over the bar. *Photo: Central Press.*

may fall only a yard or two away, he must 'follow' the line and either chase the loose ball or prepare for a follow-up save.

The other form of deflection is a *safety-first* save. 'Keepers catching a high ball should always be aware of being charged when they touch the ground. When they are close to goal, that represents serious danger, and therefore instead of catching, the 'keeper will play safe and choose to deflect it over the crossbar. It is unwise to flick the ball over the bar with the back of the hand. The palm and fingers of either both or one hand need to be used, guiding and directing the ball to safety. If possible the ball should be contacted when it is higher than the bar.

If there is any reasonable pace on the high ball near goal, whether it be shot or cross, always choose the palms and fingers. I once tried to punch a driven ball, from the former Leeds and Scotland international Peter Lorimer, over the bar. Unfortunately I

Deflecting – helping a cross on.
Photo: Syndication International.

learned a hard lesson, because by the time I had the fists clenched, the ball was touching them and flying off them into the net. Had I played safe and kept the palms and fingers forward, I guarantee I would have saved. I never repeated my foolish act!

Dealing with the low ball

The low ball crossed into the box can present just as many, if not more problems than the high ball. More decisions have to be made for a start. In the high cross it's a case of catching, punching or deflecting. With the low ball there are a minimum of six possibilities. Shown in Figure 9, they are:

1) A direct shot inside the near post. To avoid being caught and conceding a goal, a 'keeper must resist the temptation to go early. Anticipation is important, but make it too obvious to the striker and he may squeeze the ball between 'keeper and post.

2) Low driven cross three to four yards from goal. Even hit with real pace, this type of ball should be cut out by the 'keeper.

3) Pull back to six-yard line at near post. If this ball has no pace on it a 'keeper might just reach it by diving at full stretch. With reasonable pace a dive might still be on, but holding the ball would be unlikely. A really sharp pull-back and the 'keeper must either take a chance by diving lengthways across the goal-line while attempting to present a barrier, or stay on his feet in the hope of reacting to any shot which might be close to him.

4) A pull-back to the middle of the goal, twelve yards or so out, presents an easier choice. Here the 'keeper must spin from his near-post position and decide to either attack the ball and cut the

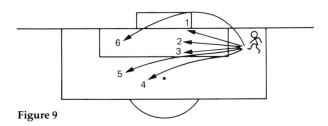

Figure 9

angle down or take a line directly across the goal which doesn't allow any narrowing of the angle, but does allow vital time to react and save by any part of the body. Personally I would recommend the latter action. At least you are buying yourself a fraction of a second longer by staying near the goal-line, and that time, little as it is, may still be enough to throw out a hand or foot.

5) Because the ball travels that bit further, the 'keeper has even more time to get into a fairly central position and possibly to narrow the angle slightly. Sharp precise footwork is essential and as in all instances the speed of the ball when hit back determines how far the 'keeper can travel both across his goal and out of it.

6) It is worth mentioning a sixth possibility, which is not a low cross but a chip to the far post. It allows just as much time for 'keepers to spin and move as the last example. Because the ball is in the air though, the 'keeper must be prepared for any eventuality, such as a diving header.

For all six possibilities a 'keeper needs to be alert, quick on his feet, composed, and capable of throwing a hand, arm, leg or foot instinctively towards a shot at goal.

The closer to goal a shot occurs from a low cross, the greater the need there is for a 'keeper to gamble, present a barrier and hope the shot strikes it. The odds are often stacked heavily in the attacker's favour and if the pitch happens to be of a greasy nature, judgement will be all the harder. There is no simple rule about diving outwards and attempting to cut out a low cross, but if in any doubt, don't go. Try instead for a brilliant reflex save from the shot which is likely to follow.

We have now covered all the major recognized saves in goalkeeping and outlined the accepted technique for each. Yet what is one 'keeper's meat may be another's poison. At the end of the day a goalkeeper's technique in any area must be assessed by the results he achieves. If he consistently prevents a breakaway forward scoring by presenting his back to the player, then that strange technique is obviously more suitable to him than an orthodox, accepted dive at feet.

When the aim is to keep the ball out of the net by any legitimate means, anything goes. It does not matter how unattractive a save appears. If it's a save it is acceptable.

Distribution

Making spectacular saves is the glamorous side of goalkeeping. Setting up attacks by a good throw or kick is the unsung side. Yet without competence in both areas a 'keeper is likely to be more of a liability than an asset. In simple terms it is pointless a 'keeper making a marvellous stop if he then clears without thought and gives the ball straight back to the opposition.

So once the 'keeper has possession of the ball, he must consider the possibilities. Not just the type of clearance to be employed, but whether he should forsake a quick clearance to enable a hard-pressed defence to recover their composure. He must give to what in effect is a pass the same tactical considerations as any outfield player. The *passes* open to a 'keeper are quite varied but can be split into different methods of:

1. *Kicking* – short, long, dead ball, half volley, etc.
2. *Throwing* – overarm, water polo, flinging, etc.

Just before I outline the technique and tactical considerations of all kicks and throws, it is perhaps advisable to enlarge a little more on the *thinking* required by a 'keeper each time he finds himself in possession. Basically he must decide on either a quick pass or a slow deliberate one.

QUICK PASS

It's fair to say that the 'keeper is in a unique position when it comes to initiating attacks. A good stop and an immediate accurate clearance can cause chaos and catch the opposition completely unawares. Although opponents obviously hold the initiative when they are on the attack, they are at the same time vulnerable should they lose possession. Attacking generally requires complete commitment throughout a team, so if the opposing 'keeper suddenly halts that attack by a save or interception, there is a moment of real psychological fear. A mixture of disappointment and disarray after failing to score leaves a side extremely vulnerable to a quick break. At this moment a quick throw or long kick by the opposing 'keeper can lead to a goal before ranks are reorganized and closed.

From the 'keeper's point of view, it is essential to forget about the glory of the moment, and assess in an instant the possibilities for attack. Composure and confidence in his kicking and throwing skills are essential.

The only time a *quick pass* should be resisted is when there has been enormous pressure on the 'keeper's team. At this time he must take it upon himself to employ what I will call a . . .

SLOW PASS

Anyone who has played the game at any level knows that evenly matched games ebb and flow. One side has a spell of domination, then the other. It is on those occasions when a side has its back to the wall, is really under the cosh, being pressured continually, that the 'keeper uses his brain. If he saves and sees an opening for attack, a difficult decision must be made – 'Do I get rid of the ball and hope the lads in a good position can attack swiftly, or do we run the risk of losing it just as quickly and then being even more disorganized and under pressure in defence?'

I say there is that decision to make, but I'm sure you can appreciate that if the circumstances are such that the defence needs a break to reorganize, then the decision is an easy one. Hang on, roll or dribble the ball to the side of the area, and only when team organization looks sound again should the ball be released. A simple case of priorities really.

Kicking

It used to be accepted that an enormous boot upfield was all that was required when kicking. Nowadays more emphasis is being put on placing and directing kicks from the ground and out of hands. See Figure 10 on page 83.

DEAD BALL KICKS

These are the least accurate, and it is quite difficult to start attacks with any degree of accuracy from them. The main objective is to get the ball straight, high and as far upfield as possible, aimed naturally at colleagues or clear space into which they can move. I know many youngsters have desperate trouble getting good distance from dead ball kicks. Don't worry over much, practice will improve but never completely cure. There will come days when for a variety of reasons your kicking from the ground lacks direction and distance.

I remember very well in the 1971 FA Cup final how Arsenal's winning goal against Liverpool occurred. No, I don't mean Charlie George's rocket shot. That was only the end product of a very poor goal kick by Ray Clemence, of all people. Ray's left-foot kick was lacking in direction and distance. It went straight to the head of Arsenal's George Graham, who was already in the Liverpool defensive half. A quick burst of inter-passing between John Radford and George and suddenly the Cup had been won and lost.

Dead ball kicking in the main should be directed to either the wing or the centre forward. The best method of taking goal kicks or any dead ball kick within the penalty area is with the instep, in the same way that forwards shoot at goal. The main difference is that you must always loft the ball and get enough height to clear opponents and colleagues, so there is not the same necessity to lean over the ball as when shooting. It is also possible to get quite a good long kick with the method used for long passing or corner kicks – with the foot inclined at an angle. The small advantage here is that the ball, in gaining more height, will curl away more.

The approach to the kick should again be a matter of personal preference. As a youngster I would take ten to twelve paces before kicking. As a professional I found four to six strides perfectly adequate. After glancing at the area that ideally you would like to reach, the approach should be completely smooth, with an increasing momentum. The run should be slightly *bent*. Good distance and power are almost impossible if the approach is straight. In fact a 'toe punt' would be the only means of gaining distance.

On contact with the ball, the head should be down, eyes on the ball, the non-kicking leg alongside and close to the ball. For the actual 'strike' the ankle must be good and firm with the toes pointed. The arms provide good balance and should be angled downwards on either side of the body. There should also be a conscious effort to get power, and once contact is made, the kicking must follow through in the same direction as the ball.

One *warning* on dead ball kicks. I have often seen outfield players called on to take this type of kick, especially at junior level. Unless there is good reason in the form of a leg injury or ankle injury to the 'keeper, it is totally unacceptable. The job is not being done properly if a 'keeper doesn't take goal kicks and opponents will be quick to spot the weakness. Never forget that if a defender takes the kick, his team is depleted and in effect one man short. It *could* mean a winger or striker being unmarked and it *does* mean that the defender will be putting the opposition in an onside position should an attack develop immediately.

Dead ball kicking isn't entirely limited to long clearances. Indeed should there be little joy or even limited joy when kicking off the ground, a *short dead ball kick* should be considered. It ensures possession being kept and should be followed by a full volleyed drop kick or one of a variety of throws.

So 'keepers must master most basic passing techniques, especially the *inside-of-the-foot pass*, so that colleagues can be found outside the penalty area. Chances should rarely be taken and only if a colleague is clearly in space, unmarked, should a quick firm pass be attempted.

The last of the dead ball kicking methods is the *short chip*. It requires the same degree of concentration as a long kick and is far more accurate. However, it requires enormous confidence on the 'keeper's part because chipping is a highly skilful technique. Misjudge height and distance and you will be in trouble very quickly.

KICKING FROM THE HAND

There are very few problems attached to kicking out of the hands. Distance is far greater than the dead ball kick, direction more easy to achieve. The only difficult decisions to be made are whether to *full-volley* or *half-volley* the ball.

The technique required when *volleying on the full* is similar to kicking a dead ball. Eye on the ball, a smooth approach, good follow-through, etc. But the major difference is that the ball is released from the hands. Personal preference comes into play as to how high the ball is tossed before striking. All I would say is that the higher the throw from the hands the greater the accuracy and timing needed to make good contact. My preference was a small, limited release, and I would strike the ball very soon after it had left the hands. What must be developed is *timing*, a real knack of bringing the swinging foot to the ball at the best moment.

Confidence, as always, plays a major part in any kick from hands, and with the full volley you can adapt it for a variety of needs; kicking for length, direction or even a combination of each.

Kicking for distance requires slightly less concentration on technique, but more power and effort. Given reasonable weather conditions it is quite possible to kick from the edge of the penalty area and, with one or two bounces, reach the other end. Kicking for direction requires more concentration on technique and less power. Aiming for heads of front men, or open spaces to the side into which they can run to meet the ball, or dropping the ball short in front of them are the three major considerations, and these kicks demand a pointed toe and a flatter trajectory than the distance kick.

Kicking for distance *and* direction is difficult but by no means impossible. In 1969 Arsenal played Tottenham Hotspur in the semi-final of the League Cup. With five minutes to go, the first leg at Highbury looked all set to be a goalless draw. I found the ball in my hands and space to kick. Spurs had retreated to a man into their defensive half but were at the same time pushing Arsenal's forwards as far from their penalty area as possible. In other words, most players from both sides were in a compact area. There was lots of space between them and Pat Jennings in the Spurs goal.

So I attacked that space, caught the ball cleanly and sent it powerfully and well directed into the night air. By the time the Spurs defenders fully realized the danger, the ball had bounced behind them, was loose and promptly met on the full by John Radford, the Arsenal striker. Jennings never had a chance. The ball nestled in the corner of the net and the one-goal lead secured was enough to see Arsenal through to Wembley, because the second leg at White Hart Lane finished 1-1.

The *half-volley* is beautiful to watch when done well but disastrous if it goes wrong. And it can and does go wrong. A very high level of skill is required to perfect a half-volley. Concentration and perfect timing can produce a lovely end-product, a ball hit with pace and a perfect trajectory. If either concentration or timing is lacking or if the ball hits a divot at the moment of contact, then direction will be lost completely and a *slice* will occur. Quite simply, if done well, half-volleying is a delightful attribute, but if you are less than happy about it, don't take a chance.

Finally, all kicking demands that the contacting foot travels as fast as possible.

The need to be two-footed Rarely is any footballer blessed with two good natural feet. One or other is generally favoured. Unfortunately in goalkeeping both are needed and consequently must be developed. They are needed because a common tactic in the game is for forwards to 'stand on' 'keepers. This means standing in front of them, blocking the way of the natural clearance.

Forwards who get to know that a 'keeper is one-footed will stand on the good side all the time. The effect on a 'keeper who doesn't feel competent with the bad foot is one of panic. He will lose composure, rush the kick and even occasionally kick the ball against a forward. Referees seem to be more in sympathy than they should be with 'keepers over this problem. Ninety-nine times out of a hundred a free kick will be awarded in the 'keeper's favour. Even I, a goalkeeper, think they are usually wrong. Unless an opponent puts his foot up or throws out an arm to deliberately block, he has not committed a foul. It should be the 'keeper's responsibility to improve his kicking well enough to clear with either foot.

THE FOUR-STEP RULE

Law 12 of the Rules of the Game concerns fouls and misconduct. Within the law is the section on the award of *indirect free kicks*, and it includes penalizing the goalkeeper if he 'takes more than four steps whilst holding, bouncing or throwing the ball in the air and catching it again without releasing it so that it is played by another player' and 'indulges in tactics which in the opinion of the Referee are designed merely to hold up the game and thus waste time and so give unfair advantage to his own team'.

Since the introduction of the four-step rule, much of the time-wasting associated with goalkeepers has been removed. He can of course still dribble the ball around his area but not to his heart's content. Opponents would be silly not to nip in and challenge. When these challenges do occur a 'keeper must be proficient at extracting himself from the tight corner.

From the outset let me impress that the greatest requirement is *acting ability*. Learning to feint to throw the ball one way, knowing that it is to be kicked on the opposite side, is essential. It's a case of *bluff*. Imagine an opponent standing directly in front of you, clearly intending to block your good kicking foot. First take stock of the situation, look your opponent straight in the eyes while holding the ball tight to your chest. He can't see what is behind him or even to the sides, so when you are ready, make a distinct movement one way as if you are going to throw the ball to some-one. Accompany this movement with a clear shout, 'John!' or whoever you like. When you do this the opponent will almost certainly follow that way. You now have him off-balance and wrong-footed. A quick turn inwards and across him and you will be clear to throw or kick. All you require is a yard.

Having done the hard work don't rush the kick, especially the one with the 'bad' foot. Greater concentration and care for technique is required. The closer you are to the goal-line the more care should be taken.

One example of the dangers of the four-step rule should clarify the problem. In the 1968 FA Cup semi-final, Leeds 'keeper Gary Sprake was forced on to his left foot at the extreme point of the eighteen-yard line on the goal-line. He cleared hastily and miscued straight to an Everton player. Sprake was then stranded when the ball was chipped towards goal, where Leeds defender Jack Charl-ton was forced to handle and concede a penalty. So Leeds were put out of the competition as a direct result of the four-step rule.

The difficulties involved are the same whether the goalkeeper is trying to *kick* or *throw*.

Throwing

Throwing the ball is far easier to master than kicking. Throws of all types should be accurate and enable the player receiving the ball to control it with ease. A 'keeper should never get into the habit of using a throw more than a kick or vice versa. If you are producing constantly successful results, by all means stick with it,

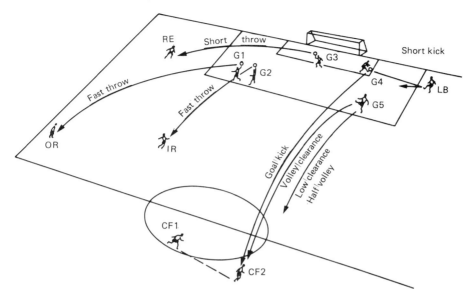

Figure 10   Different types of clearance

but normally a mixture and variety of clearance causes the opposition greater problems. See Figure 10.

The main advantage of throwing over kicking is that it ensures that a side keeps possession, and when that's the case the opposition cannot be a threat. Throwing also enables a 'keeper to change the direction of play swiftly and sharply.

There are several accepted methods of throwing a ball and the one chosen depends mainly on distance required and the position of opponents.

OVERARM THROW

The 'keeper will employ this throw when he is looking for distance. With the correct physical attributes and practice the overarm throw can travel easily as far as a dead ball kick. It is certainly likely to be more accurate. The ball is held by the hand with fingers evenly spread but strong and firm, so there is no danger of it dropping free when the arm is extended. As the body turns sideways, the arm with the ball in the hand will be extended almost fully. The action of delivery is then very similar to a bowler's action in cricket, except that the 'keeper must release the ball earlier than a bowler. He doesn't bring the arm completely over like a cricketer unless the route to his colleague is clear of opponents, which is very unlikely when distance is involved.

Strength is most important, as is a 'fast arm'. For once it's not necessary to keep an eye on the ball. It's far more important to weigh up the target and assess the strength, pace and type of trajectory required. All the power and fast delivery must occur within a maximum foot movement of four strides.

WATER POLO/JAVELIN THROW

Where distances are less, the short water polo/javelin throw is used. I call it that so you can form a mental picture of what is required. It is a quicker, sharper, more precise throw which is best used when a 'keeper is looking to find a target twenty to twenty-five yards away or less. The great advantage is the impetus that is obtained when the hand is drawn back in a straight line in the opposite direction to which it will be thrown. At the extreme backward range, the arm is fully bent. It is then brought through and at its fastest point the ball is released. The left foot is advanced so that the weight of the body is evenly distributed. The grip and contact with the fingers needs to be slightly flexible. If there is too much attention paid to finger strength, there is a chance spin can be put on the ball so that it swerves before reaching its target.

The flight of the ball should almost always be downward and aimed at feet or ground where a colleague can collect comfortably.

UNDERARM THROW

For very short distances, of say twelve to eighteen yards, it is quite acceptable to deliver the ball in an underarm manner, very similar to that used in bowls. Unlike most throws the underarm is one which delivers the ball into space slightly in front of a colleague. Delivery can be firm but, as with all football passing, the weighting of the ball is important if there is to be no delay in controlling and moving.

FLING

A fourth technique in throwing the ball is a 'flinging' movement where the arm is almost parallel with the ground. The delivery is with a fast arm across the body and the ball, once delivered, will be sure to curl away from a player in the left back position and curl in to a player in the right back position (vice versa if you are left-handed). Not many 'keepers use this method, but throughout his goalkeeping career Pat Jennings practised it with a high degree of success.

Whatever type of throw a 'keeper uses, he should take into consideration ground conditions and whether or not a call needs to accompany the throw. If the player receiving the ball has his back to an opponent he will be looking for a call to inform him whether to hold the ball, turn with it or lay it off.

The best goalkeepers put an enormous amount of thought into their distribution. Over a period of time they assess individual weaknesses so that there is no unnecessary pressure put upon any player. Similarly they weigh up the strengths of players, and if the side contains an outstanding target man or header of the ball, they deliver balls accordingly.

The Arsenal 'double' side contained two men, John Radford and Ray Kennedy, who were good both in the air for flick-ons and at offering themselves as a target. Consequently I was able to pick and choose a long punt to head, or a ball dropped short which both men held on to expertly, until support arrived.

Arthur Rowe's famous Spurs 'push and run' side based their play on never losing the ball, and Rowe insisted that possession began whenever goalkeeper Ted Ditchburn had the ball. So quick, short, accurate *throws* from Ted invariably set Spurs on the move. It is a nice irony that some fifteen or sixteen years after that Spurs side, a young Irishman called Pat Jennings, then in possession of the number one jersey, *kicked* his way into football history.

Spurs were playing Manchester United in the 1967 Charity Shield. Jennings had the ball and unleashed an enormous kick

which was simply aimed at turning the United defence and causing a chase between them and the Spurs attack. In the event the
ball dropped way beyond all of them and short of Alex Stepney in
the United goal. The goalkeeper was already off his line to anticipate any through ball, but when he realized the height and pace of
Jennings's kick he hesitated as to whether to go and meet it or
retreat. By the time he chose the latter course of action the ball had
landed and skipped over his head into the empty net. A freak goal,
but together with the short throwing of Ted Ditchburn it indicates
the extremes of distribution.

Set pieces

In this section we cover:

Free kicks

Corner kicks

Throw-ins

Penalties.

The first three of these involve a great deal of teamwork and
planning but the penalty kick is a situation where the 'keeper is
completely on his own. For the moment I would ask you to forget
the penalty completely and concentrate instead on the types of set
pieces against which it is always extremely difficult to defend.

One problem of defending at free kicks, corner kicks and even to
some extent at throw-ins comes about because the opposing side
has time to get into the penalty area in numbers. They don't just
rush into the box in any old manner but have prearranged positions according to individual strengths. The other major problem
at free kicks and corner kicks is that the defending side cannot
rush, hurry or really threaten the person delivering the ball. The
rules of the game state that the defending side must be ten yards
away from the ball. In League football the proportion of goals
scored from set pieces and dead ball situations is between fifty
and sixty per cent. A frightening statistic for the goalkeeper in
particular, and one which demands tremendous concentration
and organization from him.

Make no mistake, the basic responsibility for organizing defenders, for spotting gaps, for controlling the moment, rests with

the 'keeper. He has to go about his work quickly and confidently, know what he's doing and command complete attention and respect from his team mates. Arguments, even discussions, are out. If you argue, you waste time, lose concentration and can be made to pay for it.

Good organization at all set pieces only comes from practice, and time must be set aside at training sessions for this purpose.

Free kicks

THE 'KEEPER'S COURSE OF ACTION

1) Immediately a direct free kick is conceded around the penalty area the 'keeper must forget all complaints of injustice and, more important, stop his colleagues from wasting valuable time complaining. Referees rarely change their minds about free kick decisions.

2) Start by getting the nearest man to stand in line with the ball, ten yards away from it. At least you have a one-man barrier of protection to help you immediately. Even one man can threaten and challenge for the ball if a short free kick is taken. His presence may also be enough to prevent a direct shot on goal.

3) This is of course emergency action only, and within seconds the one-man wall must become two, three, four or five men, depending on where the free kick is to be taken from. This is outlined shortly.

The 'keeper's view of a free kick through a wall (Brazil *v.* Czechoslovakia, World Cup, 1970). *Photo: Syndication International.*

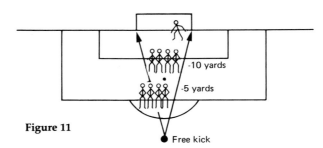

Figure 11

Free kick

4) Work in cooperation with one outfield player in whom you have complete confidence. Leave him the job of *lining* the wall on whatever side you desire so that you can concentrate all the time on defending the exposed side of goal.

5) As soon as the free kick is conceded the keeper must decide how many men he requires in the wall and one hand must be raised showing two, three, four or five fingers accordingly.

6) Insist the wall is set ten yards from the kick. There are more problems than benefits from encroaching five yards from the ball. The wall will inevitably be moved the statutory ten yards by the referee anyway, and if that happens after the lining-up and adjusting has been completed, gaps may easily appear and angles could be fractionally astray. In Figure 11 the wall at five yards obviously covers the goal adequately. Move it back to ten yards and it is vulnerable.

7) Although it is the keeper's basic responsibility to organize those in front of him, *lining* up the wall is *not* his main concern. Defending the goal *is*, and he need only *check* that he's happy with the position of the wall, and then only if time permits.

So at all free kicks the goalkeeper needs to rely on a well marshalled team who help to protect his two main interests, covering the side of the goal that the 'keeper is not covering, and allowing the 'keeper a clear view of the ball.

THE GOALKEEPER'S POSITION

A clear view of the ball is essential if a 'keeper is to dive and save or react to a clip or lob. So his position should be to the side of the

A five-man wall lined up for a free kick (West Germany *v*. England, 1978). *Photo: Colorsport.*

wall, never behind it. The best advice I can give is to suggest he takes up a position that in effect would represent an extra man in the wall, only he stays on his line or a yard off it. See Figure 12. If a 'keeper moves too far to the side of the wall he becomes vulnerable to a shot bent round the wall and a chip over it. He will then have a lot of ground to make up, possibly too much.

Other tips you may find useful:

1) Stay low and in contact with the ground, so that there is no chance of being caught on an upward bounce. In other words don't jump about in an excited, agitated fashion.

2) You can tuck yourself in closer to the side of the wall if you angle the top half of the body and adopt a 'peep-around' pose. As long as you are comfortable and can see the ball, that is all that matters.

3) Give a confident appearance from the moment a free kick is awarded against you – calm, cool, controlled. You would be surprised how much such an appearance causes opponents to change their mind.

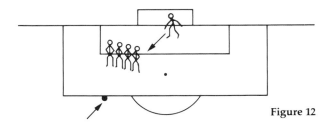

Figure 12

4) A 'keeper's position in relation to the goal-line depends on where the free kick is. Eighteen or twenty yards or so from goal and he can afford to be a couple of yards from his line, but the closer to goal a free kick is, the more need the 'keeper has to buy himself time to react to a shot, chip or lob. Stand on the line if the free kick is really close.

NUMBER OF PLAYERS IN A WALL

As already mentioned, the number of players in a wall depends entirely on where the free kick takes place. It is silly to put too many players in a wall if the angle from which the kick is being taken is narrow. It is also dangerous, because all set pieces require as much consideration for marking players as for marking space. It is no good having a perfectly placed wall and leaving three or four opponents unmarked in dangerous positions. In simple terms, a six-man wall leaves a potential threat of nine attackers against your other four colleagues.

Deciding on the correct number of players in a wall is not really a problem at all. There are simple guidelines which have stood the test of time: see Figure 13.

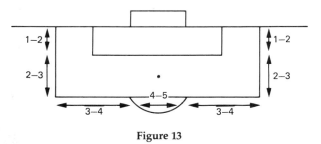

Figure 13

Two-man wall
For the free kick at a fairly acute angle only two defenders are necessary. The same principles apply, in that the outside man

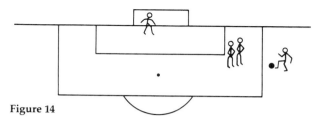

Figure 14

needs to be lined up a yard outside the near post. See Figure 14. The two men are simply preventing an attacker with a strong shot from blasting or bending a kick straight at goal. It is almost foolproof and opponents know it. On ninety per cent of occasions the free kick will become a pass or cross chip.

Two- or three-man wall
Exactly the same applies to the two- or three-man wall for free kicks from the edge of the penalty area as with the one- or two-man wall at the more acute angle, and generally with as much success in preventing direct shots at goal.

Three- or four-man wall
This free kick represents much more of a threat and calls for a strong line-up. Ideally the four men in the wall should comprise the player responsible for lining the wall, a midfield player and two forwards. They should be close together so that there is no possibility of the wall breaking. See Figure 15.

The 'keeper must not be content to believe that the wall is impregnable. He must be on the alert to cover any ball that gets through or to the side of the wall, any chip or lob over the wall and a bender round the wall.

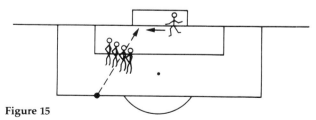

Figure 15

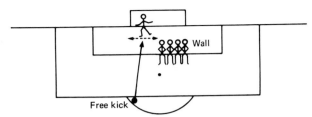

Figure 16

There is an alternative three- or four-man line-up to the one just outlined. I include it out of respect and admiration for Jack Kelsey, the former great 'keeper of Wales and Arsenal. Jack's three- or four-man wall for free kicks in front of goal at an angle reversed positions completely. The wall covered the far side of the goal where the 'keeper normally stands in the more readily accepted method, and the 'keeper in turn took the more obvious gap directly in line with the ball (see Figure 16). On paper it appears a dangerous method, and it can't be denied that the 'keeper is encouraging a direct shot at goal, but Jack Kelsey will tell you that in the whole of his illustrious career he only conceded one free-kick goal when employing this technique.

Four- or five-man wall
For the free kick which is taken in a central position, it is advisable to erect a five-man wall which can be in the form of a complete unit as in Figure 17, or a split five-man wall as in Figure 18.

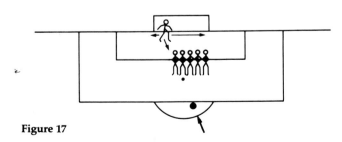

Figure 17

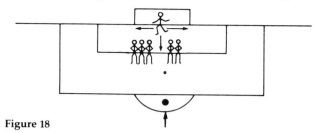

Figure 18

Personal preference again comes into play. I was happier with the complete five-man unit and got edgy on the few occasions I tried the split wall. The main reason for my concern was the number of deflections which came off the inside men in the split wall.

Advice to walls If as 'keeper you see players in the wall linking arms or putting arms around each other's waist, stop them immediately. A lot of free kicks cannon off walls or other defending players. The men in the wall should be as free as possible, so that they can react in a variety of ways once the kick has been taken.

All in all, walls must stand up, make themselves as big and as formidable a barrier as possible, and be brave.

POSITIONING OF OTHER DEFENDERS

Clearly the ten-yard rule prevents every opponent being marked, but whenever opponents take up a position in the box, then they require *marking* by the members of the team not involved in the wall. Such is the danger from free kicks that often all eleven members of the defending side need to be back helping. The 'free' men must include the best defenders, men capable of reading tactics and clever set plays.

There are two or three other situations when the 'keeper must ensure that his side are well drilled.

For a *free kick in the 'D'* the whole team is needed to help out, five in the wall, five deployed in the box, with one or two of the latter to the side of the ball (see Figure 19 overleaf), so that if it is played short, they can *threaten* the kicker.

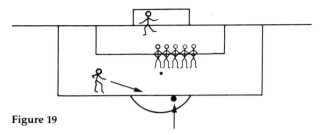

Figure 19

For a *free kick in front of goal* but at an angle, the two players who can be threatened most are (1) the full back who has to guard against the threat from an attack down the flank and (2) the central defender who has to be able to match opposing defenders and attackers in the air, for a chip free kick. See Figure 20.

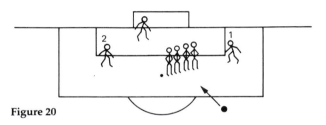

Figure 20

For a *free kick to the side*, even more space is threatened, and the most often exploited space is the near post. As the ball doesn't travel very far, a great deal of anticipation, speed and courage is needed by the defender. See Figure 21.

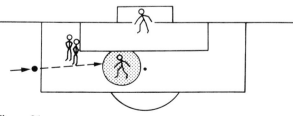

Figure 21

INDIRECT FREE KICKS CLOSE TO GOAL

There is one other free kick situation for which an emergency plan must be prepared in detail. It is when an indirect free kick has been awarded a matter of yards from the goal-line. There is only one accepted method of defence here and that is for the 'keeper to collect all ten other colleagues, who join him on the goal-line to form an eleven-man human barrier. It looks ungainly, causes much amusement to spectators but is very effective. In the whole of my career I do not recall any side that I played for conceding a goal from a close-range free kick. In fact, when I was taking my FA Full Badge Award, we experimented and in the space of a couple of hours failed to get the ball in the back of the net once, against an eleven-man barrier.

The goalkeeper's position at this type of set piece should be a central one, in line with the ball. Really he needs to be the closest defender to the ball simply because he has an advantage over colleagues as the ball is played. The 'keeper can dive, block, or simply distract the kicker, although I must admit that at times doing so requires extremes of courage.

Corner kicks

If a 'keeper takes on a captain's role when free kicks are awarded around the box, then it's a major's command which is required from him after a corner is conceded.

There are many times when playing in goal that *acting* ability helps. It's certainly the case at corner kicks. The percentage of goals scored from them is frighteningly high, and you can't ignore that, but you can fight it with a cool, calculating head and a combination of skill and courage.

The opposition get the bit between their teeth when they win a corner. They sense a goal and will send troops into the battle area at the expense of protecting their own defensive lines. It is easy to become confused and anxious about the number of bodies, both friend and foe, who pack into the penalty area. At such times the 'keeper must organize himself and his team in a well rehearsed manner.

THIS PAGE AND OPPOSITE Corner kicks: it is easy for the 'keeper to become confused and anxious about the number of bodies, both friend and foe, who pack into the penalty area. *Photos: Press Association, Associated Press and Colorsport.*

1) Get one or two team mates swiftly into position inside each post.

2) See that the near post area is well defended.

3) Clear the six-yard box in front of you of all colleagues, and don't stand for any argument even if it leaves you outnumbered by opponents.

4) Make the order to 'clear decks' loudly, confidently and in a *threatening* manner – 'John, get out to the six-yard line – leave *him* to me!' If you get so much as a surprised glance from the opponent, you are on your way to competing on level terms.

5) Take a final glance at the defensive organization and then be as bouncy on your feet as you want to be. When the ball is out wide, remember you have time to react to anything, and it sometimes helps 'keepers to be alive, bouncy and alert. Once preparations are completed, the 'keeper's next task is to instil in himself an iron will and resolution not to fail, because coming up will be one of a variety of uncomfortable man-to-man confrontations. Here are the possibilities:

SHORT CORNER

As long as the defending team has equal numbers with the opponents there should be little problem. Therefore if the opposition place two players with the ball in the corner, the defending team must counter it and ensure they also have two players threatening.

NEAR POST CORNER

Without question the corner aimed to a head at the near post is the most difficult to defend. There will always be one opponent who possesses unerring accuracy with a chipped pass.

The main aim of this corner is to cause confusion, although goals have often been scored directly from the head of the opponent at the near post. It can be either an intended or unintentional attempt at goal, but either way, if the initial cross has pace on it, the ball can fly. The trouble, from the goalkeeper's point of view, is that you can't anticipate or predict at what angle it will leave an opponent's head.

It is also possible, even probable, that because of the congestion in front of the near post, it could be one of the 'keeper's own players who gets the last touch. Much effort and straining of neck muscles is involved from members of both sides, and a well placed chip could find any one of five or six heads. Therefore the 'keeper should be on his toes to:
1) Keep the direct header out of the net.
2) Anticipate the flick-on to the middle of goal.
3) Spin and adjust position for a firm flick to the far post which can't be intercepted.
He should *not* attempt to clamber over a mass of bodies at the near post and try to punch unless he has an outstanding chance of getting there first.

It is not good enough to go and do battle, only to be left stranded. You would be better playing safe, staying around the line and reacting to the touch on. It is a different matter when the ball is curled in really high and close to the near post. Unless you attack this corner kick you stand to be beaten directly by the inswinger, with no one touching the ball at all. See Figure 22.

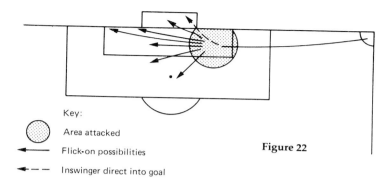

Key:

Area attacked

Flick-on possibilities

Figure 22

Inswinger direct into goal

MIDDLE GOAL CORNER

Depending on the type of cross struck, the 'keeper will be expected to dominate completely the corner kick aimed to mid-goal –
see Figure 23. If it is a cross without pace he should be competing
to catch or punch right up to the penalty spot, i.e. twelve yards.

There will be nothing easy about the mid-goal corner. It will be
an out-and-out battle requiring a quick decision to catch or
punch. All I would implore is that the battle is between you and
the opposition. If your own players are involved you are only
making life difficult for yourself.

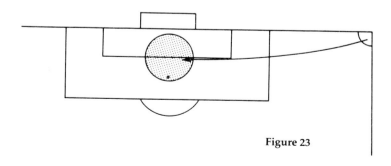

Figure 23

FAR POST CORNER

Unlike the mid-goal corner, there are more than two basic decisions for a 'keeper to make when the ball is floated or driven to the
far post (see Figure 24). He can go out and attack the cross, stay on
the goal line, catch, punch or deflect. Even then there are extra
technical decisions to make if the impulse is to go for the cross.

The major difference the 'keeper faces with the far post corner is
that he has to travel sideways or backwards rather than being able
to move forward as in the near post and mid-goal cross. The major
problem is that he will often be 'blind' to bodies behind him. All
the solid techniques listed in the section on the high cross are
called for – little mincing steps, a compact body, preparedness for
a challenge.

If a catch is made, it is almost certain that the 'keeper will need
to go to ground. He will be off-balance and open to challenge still.
By going to ground the possibility of the ball being knocked out of
his grasp will be reduced.

If the 'keeper decides to punch, it will invariably be a 'help-on'
type of connection, the fist making contact and helping the ball
continue in the direction it is going, but on a higher plane.

Where the 'keeper goes and struggles to punch or catch, he can
call on the 'deflected' type of save, which is an open hand turning
the ball away from immediate danger. This calls for alertness and
expectancy of a quick return shot, since the deflecting distance
will not be as great as with a punch.

Whatever type of corner, the defending of it is not a one-man

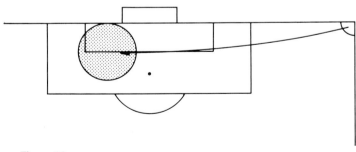

Figure 24

effort. The goalkeeper will hope to dominate the situation but he needs help and an assurance of mind that should he only half clear, the alertness of his colleagues will complete the clearance. So the *positioning* and *organization* at corner kicks must be practised as often as the free-kick situations.

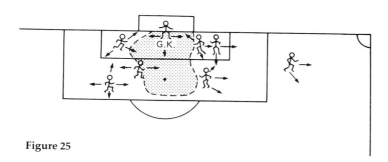

Figure 25

Figure 25 illustrates the most important areas which need to be covered. The number of players involved is seven not counting the 'keeper. That leaves three players, two of whom can be given a free role. By this I mean they can be used wherever most danger threatens. They should be 'bossed' by the 'keeper and directed to defend a vulnerable area. One and sometimes two players should be well out of the penalty area, threatening a quick attack if possession is won. It is silly to pull all eleven players into the penalty area. All it does is encourage ten opponents to attack.

THE GOALKEEPER'S BASIC POSITION

The possibilities at corner kicks are clearly numerous. Near post, mid-goal, far post, penalty spot, etc. I hate, as you know, to lay down hard-and-fast rules, but the goalkeeper's starting position at corner kicks is one I would be prepared to argue about passionately.
   The demands are so great that there is only one position which gives the 'keeper a chance of covering every possibility. It is a position *slightly backward of central,* closer to the back post than the

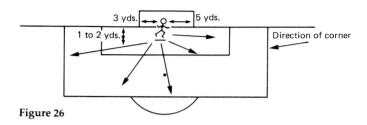

Figure 26

near post – see Figure 26. The only reason that it is not exactly central is because the far post cross requires sideways and backward movement, which is not as fast as a forward movement. There can be more adaptability regarding the distance the 'keeper stands off his line. In theory two yards out from goal is a sound starting position. It enables a 'keeper to travel further for a cross than if he was on the goal-line, and it is not too far out should he need to tip an inswinger over the bar.

A number of opponents standing in front of the 'keeper will often determine how far out he stands, so hard-and-fast rules are impossible. Mention of those awkward men who stand 'on the goalkeeper' is a nice way to bring this section on corners to a close. Yes, they are a threat, they can be awkward, they are a menace, they are likely to be clumsy, *but* they are also only human. When they come into that six-yard line they are full of confidence, but that confident, threatening shout I told you about – 'Get out of the way, John, leave them to me!' – if not scaring them to death, will at least cause them to look over their shoulder.

The long throw-in

There is no need to dwell on the problems caused by a long throw-in, or indeed the methods of dealing with them. The problems are exactly the same as those caused by the near post corner and the mid-goal corner.

The one major difference involves the 'keeper's starting position. Instead of being slightly off-centre, he needs to be much closer to the near post. Very few players are capable of throwing in and reaching the far post, and the majority are aiming for that near post area, seeking the head of a colleague who can flick the ball on or direct it outwards to a waiting striker.

The only real tip I can pass on from my experience is that you will often be able to commit yourself to going for the initial throw-in. The pace of the ball is altogether slower than from a corner kick. That being the case, there is *time* to get to where the ball is directed as well as calling to defenders and getting them out of the way. You might not always be able to catch, but a punch which halts the initial threat is still better than an unpredictable flick-on header from an opponent.

Penalties

What a delightful way to bring this particular section on set pieces, and the complete chapter on techniques, to an end – the death-or-glory area of a penalty kick!

The tension when a spot kick is about to be taken is quite indescribable. It is a supreme moment, incorporating skill and nerve, for both the *player who has to score* and the *'keeper who isn't really expected to save.*

Maybe I've surprised you again with part of that last statement but it is absolutely fact that if a penalty kick is properly placed and correctly struck there is no man on earth who can stop it – *legally*. In fact I'll go further than that, and suggest that only one per cent of penalty saves by goalkeepers have been legal.

I can hear you saying: 'Whose side are you on?' Well, I'm on the goalkeeper's side of course, but I want to see fair play and consistency on the part of referees, not the widely differing interpretation of the rules as they have stood for many years. It's not really the referee's fault but an impossible rule. Let's look at the part of it which concerns the goalkeeper:

Law 14 – penalty kick
' . . . the opposing goalkeeper must stand (without moving his feet) on his own goal-line, between the goalposts until the ball is kicked . . . '
' . . . the ball shall be deemed in play directly it is kicked, i.e. travelled the distance of its circumference . . . '

Graham Rix is un-
successful with a
penalty kick
(Arsenal *v.* Valencia.
European Cup
Winners' Cup final,
1980).
Photo: Colorsport.

In other words a goalkeeper cannot, strictly speaking, move his feet
at all on or off the line until a ball is nearly one yard away from the
kicker's foot. It's laughable, and I smile to myself every time I see a
'keeper save. He has really saved by a mixture of breaking the
rules and a non-application of them by the referee.

You might say: 'It's only a referee using his common sense.' I
would agree with you except that some referees do apply common
sense and others interpret the laws literally. It is nonsense to
expect a 'keeper, entrusted with the job of stopping a goal, to keep
his feet motionless until the ball is on its way. The only way he
would save in this instance is if the ball was directed straight at
him.

The answer? A change in the rule which allows the 'keeper to
move should he wish, and take a chance, but not with a forward

movement. The reason for the latter point is that many 'keepers already hurl themselves forward off the line to distract and attempt to narrow the angle. If he was allowed to do this after the whistle had been blown for a kick to be taken, he could be nearly at the penalty taker's feet. Allowing the 'keeper to move early on the line would eliminate argument about the legality of a kick, and the 'keeper would stand a very big risk of going too early and leaving one corner of the goal empty.

A controversial suggestion? Possibly so, but surely a vast improvement on the contradictory nature of the penalty kick as it has stood through the years. Anyway, back to the problems a 'keeper faces and the methods he can adopt when the referee points to the spot.

'Penalty!' Referees rarely change their mind once they've awarded a penalty so unless there is a very good reason to contest the decision, the 'keeper must resist the temptation to wave his arms, lose his head and rush around in a temper. Every second is valuable before the kick is taken to enter into *psychological warfare* with the penalty taker.

The most important thing is not to let him have it easy. He'll want to get the ordeal over as quickly as possible. The 'keeper can make it even more of an ordeal by delaying tactics. Showing ignorance of the rules and standing a couple of yards off the goal-line is one way. The referee will soon push you back anyway.

If there is any loose paper or suchlike lying in the goalmouth, go over and pick it up, but take your time doing it. The longer it takes for the kick to be taken the more doubts will enter the taker's head. If you have the nerve to do it, get into a set position and just as the referee is about to blow the whistle, put up your arms and make out that something has caught your eye and you're not ready. It might be an opponent encroaching into the penalty area.

The man we goalkeepers have to blame for the restrictions in movement placed upon us is one Rab McFarland, who evidently would stand on his line and, as the opponent ran up to kick the ball, would tear off his cap, whirl it round and bawl the most frightening gibberish. He also danced around to such an extent that the kicker was put off. So famous did this 'gift' become that the rule as it stands today had to be drawn up.

KICKER'S APPROACH

Now to the more technical side of penalty kicks – assessing the direction of the shot. The run-up of the taker can occasionally give a clue. For instance if the run is quite a quick one there's a good chance the kicker is relying on pace to beat you – a real 'blasted' penalty.

If the taker is clearly right-footed, then the natural thing for him to do is to follow the natural line of the swing, so this would be a shot to the 'keeper's right. Kickers who run in an arc towards the ball will again be likely to shoot with their natural follow-through. If the approach is a straight one, stay on your feet as long as possible, because the kicker will have to make some late angle for himself.

Personally I wouldn't read too much into the approach run. I think it is far preferable to take the initiative yourself and try to create doubt in the kicker's mind, outwit him or simply guess correctly.

SAVING PENALTIES

Coming up is a list of the possibilities for pulling off a penalty save. The essential ingredient is confidence in knowing what you are going to attempt. If you change your mind at the last moment you will fail as surely as the penalty taker who changes his mind at the last moment.

1) *Taking a chance* is the favourite method in use. Here the 'keeper, either with previous knowledge of the kicker or simply instinct, has his mind totally tuned to diving one way or another. When it works it has spectacular results, a save of almost unbelievable proportions. However, in all honesty the percentage of success is small.

2)   *Staying upright* has an equally low success rate. The advantage of staying on the feet and not committing yourself early is that any miscued shot or blaster at the middle of the goal is likely to be saved. Lots of times you must have seen goalkeepers commit themselves and dive for a corner, only for the ball to enter the goal at the very spot in the middle of the goal they had just vacated.

One such case which I will never forget was in the 1971 FA Cup semi-final when Arsenal met Stoke. Arsenal, trailing 2-1, were awarded a penalty in the last minute of the game. In goal for Stoke was Gordon Banks, at the peak of his form. Taking the penalty kick for Arsenal, Peter Storey. Try and imagine the tension and pressure on those two men, particularly Storey, who had the responsibility of giving his side a second chance of reaching the final at Wembley.

What happened serves as a perfect illustration of the chance nature of the penalty kick. Banks made up his mind to move early to his right, to take a chance, to gamble all. It wasn't a flat-out dive, but a transferring of weight to the right side, in preparation of a dive. Storey knew where he wanted to put the kick – to the 'keeper's left – but he didn't connect as he would have wished, and the direction was poor, about a couple of yards to Banks's left. It was easily savable for a 'keeper who had stayed upright: even an outstretched boot would have stopped the shot.

A penalty kick by Arsenal's Peter Storey beats Stoke City's Gordon Banks in the 1971 FA Cup semi-final. *Photo: Press Association.*

So unfortunately for Gordon Banks the decision to take a chance backfired on him. With the whole weight of his body committed to the right, he could do nothing but glance back over his shoulder as the ball crossed the line two or three yards to the left of him.

3)   *Standing to one side* is a psychological method of attempting to save a penalty. The 'keeper stands to save a penalty off-centre, favouring one side totally. In effect he is inviting the penalty taker to shoot for the big space knowing that he himself will be diving that way. It is a method which does put some doubt in the taker's mind, and that in itself is useful. Against that, a well-struck shot for the big space will still be too fast for a 'keeper to reach.

4)   *Diving to one side and moving forwards* is intended to panic the kicker, and to try to make the goal look a fraction smaller. In practice it is a most difficult penalty save, simply because saving any shot while still moving in a forward plane is extremely awkward.

All four methods mentioned so far have advantages and disadvantages. All can work occasionally, but I would recommend a method passed on to me by Alan Ball when he was playing at Arsenal.

5) *The Bally method* – Bally had watched me at penalty kicks and told me that I was very readable, very obvious and too predictable. The first thing he did was to put me into his shoes as a penalty taker. He said: 'When I run up to shoot, I'm concentrating on the ball, but I can still see the 'keeper on the edge of my vision. If he moves really early as you do, I still have a chance to adjust and play it in the empty corner. What I'm saying is that a penalty taker sees a 'keeper's movement, however hard he is concentrating on his kick. Why don't you make a clear movement with the arms one way, but stay balanced on your feet and at the last moment go the opposite way?'

I thought hard about Alan Ball's advice and started experimenting in training. Every time the kicker approached the ball, I would make a very exaggerated movement one way or the other with my arms and the top half of my body. All the time my feet remained firmly planted on the line, perfectly balanced, under control, and poised to move in the opposite direction.

At the moment the ball was struck, all my balance was immediately transferred and effort was put into diving the other way.

The great hope was that the kicker picked up the early movement in his peripheral vision, assumed I was going that way and decided to strike for the other corner.

Imagine my delight when shortly after receiving Alan Ball's advice, Arsenal played at Southampton on Boxing Day morning, and I saved a Mick Channon penalty in exactly this manner. As I lay on the floor with the ball safely turned to the side for a corner, all I could hear was Bally's familiar squeaky voice above me shouting: 'I told you so! I told you so!'

I was thirty-one when I made that penalty save. Time was beginning to run out for me in my goalkeeping career and yet there I was perfecting *a new technique*. It impressed upon me two things: one, that you should never stop learning, listening or experimenting; and two, that technique in goalkeeping is not simply a matter of putting into practice all the accepted methods recommended and passed on from generation to generation. To that sound knowledge must be added improvisation, adaptability, ingenuity, impulse.

The *accepted* plus the *acceptable* must add up to *inspiration*, which is the ultimate aim of the goalkeeper.

Dickie Guy saves Peter Lorimer's penalty kick (FA Cup fourth round, 1975).

Photo: Colorsport

5

The greatest save
'A salmon's leap'

Who is the best-ever striker? What was the best goal ever scored? Who is the greatest captain of all time? ... Arguments about the best or greatest of anything are always interesting but generally futile. There is, however, one goalkeeping save which is as vivid to me now as when I witnessed it.

The date was 7 June 1970. The goalkeeper was Gordon Banks of England. The save, his astonishing stop from a perfect header by Pele during the World Cup match in Guadalajara, Mexico. As far as I'm concerned it is the greatest save I have ever seen and arguably the greatest save of all time. Shortly I will dissect the Banks save for you and analyse its true greatness. But first, a variety of descriptions follow which help to recreate the moment for you.

Only Gordon Banks could have made the miraculous save from Pele's header that came in the 10th minute of the game. The groundwork was done by Jairzinho. Brushing past left back Cooper, the winger dashed to the line and centred perfectly. Pele headed the ball down hard, on the bounce, inside the left-hand post, and was already shouting 'Goal!' when Banks, with incredible gymnastic agility, somehow launched himself across his goal from the opposite post, to flail the ball, one-handed, over the bar.

Brian Glanville, *Sunday Times History of the World Cup*.

Instantly the game switched to the other end and Banks made the save which will never be forgotten. Jairzinho beat Cooper on the outside, cut in to the line and centred back and beyond the far post. Pele was waiting, coiled like a spring beyond

110

Mullery. Taking off with perfect timing, Pele climbed up and up, seemed to hang in the air waiting, and then with a fearsome snap from the waist, headed down for the near post. It seemed a goal all the way, but somehow Banks, twisting back and down, reached the ball as it bounced inches in front of the goal-line and punched it up and round the post. It was a feat of agility difficult to believe.

David Miller, *World Cup 1970.*

The game had not been in progress very long when we knew our worries about England were fully justified. I had this excellent opportunity to score. Jairzinho took the ball in a rush past Cooper, the strong England back, and sent it to me in a perfect high pass. I leaped for it and headed it perfectly towards one corner of the net while Banks, the English goalkeeper, was at the other corner. I was already shouting Goooaaalllll!!!! when Banks, like a salmon leaping up a falls, threw himself in the air and managed to tip the ball so that it slid over the crossbar! It was, in my opinion, the most spectacular save of the tournament, an impossible play – but Banks made it.

Edson Arantes de Nascimiento (Pele), *Pele, My Life and the Beautiful Game.*

I can remember the move starting with a pass from Carlos Alberto that was like nothing I had ever seen before. He struck the ball with the outside of his right foot from just beyond his penalty area and it swerved right round our left back, Terry Cooper, and into the path of the sprinting Jairzinho. Terry had been left for dead. Tostao, a smooth sophisticated player, came to the near post and I went with him as I sensed that Jairzinho would try to find him with a diagonal pass. What I didn't see was Pele running beyond his marker Alan Mullery at the far post. Jairzinho lofted a dipping centre high in the direction of Pele and I suddenly had to scamper back across my goal. Pele got above the ball and powered it low and hard towards the corner of the net. It was the perfect header. I was now into a dive to my right and as the ball hit the ground just in front of the goal-line I flicked it with my outstretched right hand as it came up and managed to divert it over the bar. Alan Mullery told me later that Pele had been shouting 'Goal' as I reached the ball and Pele himself was generous enough to tell me he considered it the greatest save he had ever seen.

Gordon Banks, *Banks of England.*

'The greatest' Pele had ever seen, 'the best' I have ever seen. Well, I know millions will share those sentiments, as well as having their own particular memory of Gordon Banks's *magical save.*

Describing it as magical is appropriate but inaccurate. Magic involves sleight of hand, and clever tricks of the trade. There was neither sleight of hand nor clever trick involved in Gordon's save. What was involved was year upon year of dedication in training and season upon season of concentration in games.

This man who defied the great Pele was the same man whose goal I stood behind as a youngster in Chesterfield. There was only a year or two's difference in ages between us, but I had stayed on at school and Gordon, who came from Sheffield, was just setting out on a professional career in the game with Chesterfield in what was known then as the Third Division North. In those early days I rated him full of potential but a 'flash monkey'. We've talked about it since and Gordon agrees with that assessment – 'I admit I sometimes tended to be spectacular for the sake of it.'

How quickly he learned, developed and improved as he moved from Chesterfield to Leicester and then on to Stoke. In all 'Banksy' played seventy-three times for England between 1963 and 1967, a record for a goalkeeper. During that time he was on the losing side just nine times and conceded just fifty-seven goals; an average of 0.78 goals against per game.

The game against Brazil in which he made his staggering save from Pele was number sixty-one. You've read accounts of it from four viewpoints – the two journalists, the opponent Pele, the striker, and Banks the 'keeper. My analysis is slightly less dramatic, but more objective. It is a critical dissection from a goalkeeper's point of view. There were five stages to the save.

The approach Gordon's concentration was excellent as Carlos Alberto hit a glorious forward pass with the outside of his foot. The pass hardly rose from the turf, but any inclination the 'keeper

OPPOSITE Two moments during Banks's astonishing save.
Photos: Keystone.

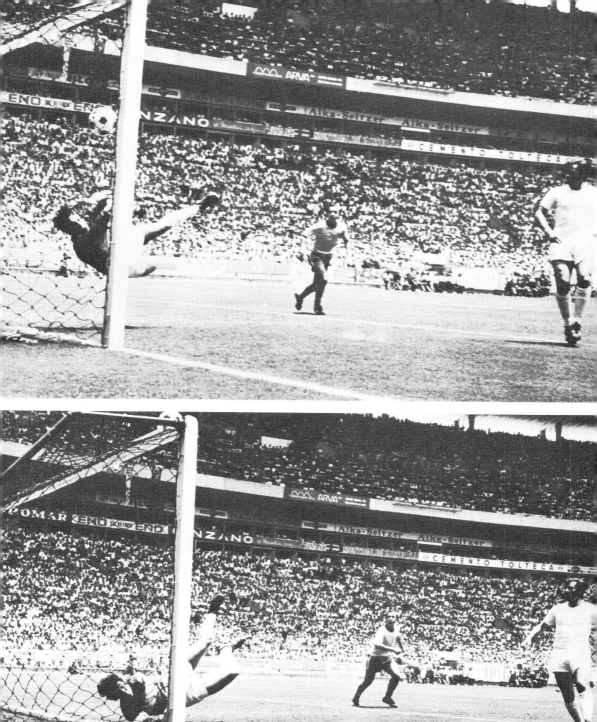

might have had to anticipate the ball on the edge of the box was forgotten, with the curl it also had on it. It took the ball away from goal rather than towards it and found space just ahead of Jairzinho. Had the 'keeper rushed from goal, he definitely wouldn't have reached the ball first, and anyway Terry Cooper was not beaten at this stage.

Covering the near post   A moment or two later, though, and Jairzinho had cut across the full back beautifully and was one yard off the goal-line and seventeen yards from the near post. Banks's starting position, two or three yards off his line and a yard inside the goal, was now vulnerable, unless he adjusted and took a pace or two diagonally backwards to cover any shot inside the near post.

Again the position of the 'keeper was correct, fractionally beyond the post so that he wouldn't collide with it if called upon to save. Once Jairzinho had achieved space to cross, Banks's goalkeeping instinct, experience and knowledge told him there were six possibilities on – the direct shot; a low driven cross to pounce on; a low pull-back to the six-yard line; a deeper angled pull-back to the middle of the goal; a driven low cross to the far post; or a chip to the far post.

His immediate concern had to be a direct shot. Next came the possibility that Tostao, who was on the near post, would be the target. His worst fear was a chip to the far post. A second later and Gordon's worst fear was realized.

The cross   As soon as Jairzinho chipped for the far post, Banks was put in a seemingly helpless position. Some 'keepers might well have surrendered, but not the England 'keeper. The reason for the desperate situation was eight yards of ground. That is the distance from post to post. Banks was therefore eight yards from where the ball was aimed, the head of Pele.

The fact that the ball was in the air was a help. It permitted the 'keeper more time than a driven cross, but only about a second more. In that time Banks managed to spin from the near post and get in four very short movements with the feet. It took him to approximately halfway across the goal, a yard from the line. As he reached this position the ball was poised to strike Pele's head at the far post, the Brazilian having outmanoeuvred Alan Mullery.

The header   Pele was seven yards from goal when he powered his header down towards goal. He was so sure he had time to pick his spot that he hung in the air and drew his head back. Had he simply attacked the cross and directed it at the target, it is extremely unlikely that Gordon would have had time to make up the ground or react to make a save. At this point of contact the goalkeeper at last knew fully what ground he still had to make up, if the header was in the bottom corner – three to four yards in which footwork had no place at all.

The save   Once Pele's header was on its way, directed perfectly into the corner, and with pace, there was only one alternative left to Gordon Banks – to hurl himself the remaining three or four yards. What was so staggering about his goalkeeping instinct was that he dived diagonally backwards. Had he dived directly toward the ball, it would almost certainly have hit the floor in front of him and bounced over his arm into the net. By diving backwards towards the goalpost, he bought himself another fraction of a second during which time the ball struck the ground a yard in front of him and bounced sharply upwards.

After that it was a case of pure goalkeeping instinct and razor-sharp reflexes as his right hand caught the ball and helped it on its upward way, only on a change of course. For a heart-stopping moment it seemed to hover near the top corner before curling over the bar. Banks himself finished wrapped around the goalpost.

All that was left was one amazed Brazilian superstar, thousands of disbelieving fans, a relieved Alan Mullery who ruffled Banks's hair as he rose, and an admiring Bobby Moore, the England skipper, who simply stood and applauded.

The five stages of Banksy's super save from Carlos Alberto's pass to the ball clearing the bar took precisely eight seconds, and it contained the following goalkeeping attributes: concentration, anticipation, good footwork, agility, composure, courage, instinct, great reactions and confidence.

It also contained humility and modesty, because when I asked Gordon about the importance of the save he told me: 'It came at a crucial time, the score was nil-nil, the lads were playing exceptionally well in the heat of the day. 102 degrees was recorded inside the stadium which obviously suited Brazil, not us. We've never had much success against them, but we were fighting hard to get a result. I don't think the lads would have stopped trying had it gone in but heads might have dropped a little at that early stage of the game.'

'Let's just say it was an important save at an important time.'

It was a similar modesty that endeared Gordon Banks, OBE, to millions. Whenever the 1972 Footballer of the Year had success, it seemed the whole nation laughed with him. When fate so cruelly ended his career prematurely, the same folk cried for him.

Whether Banksy was the greatest ever, or whether his save from Pele was the best, matters not. What is really important is that his save set goalkeepers everywhere new targets at which to aim, a new standard to try and emulate, a new save to reproduce.

It also helped to know that the 'King' was once a 'flash monkey'.

6

The elements
and outside influences

Since its early beginnings football has changed dramatically.
There are very few areas of the game which haven't been tampered
with or changed completely. Rules have been amended, training
has become sophisticated, commercialization and sponsorship
have made the game big business.

Still, whatever the changes and modifications, football remains
an outdoor pursuit, and although artificial surfaces do exist
around the world, most pitches are set out on natural surfaces.
Unfortunately, being open to the elements the condition of all
pitches varies dramatically. One day you can be playing on lush
green grass with the sun shining and three days later you might be
performing on a mudheap with rain driving into your face.

The object of this chapter is to forewarn about these dramatic
extremes of climate and ground conditions. The fact that all four
seasons have to be included is further indication of the growth of
the game. Once it was played seriously during the autumn, winter
and spring. Now football is a twelve-month pursuit.

Summer

This is one period of the year when there should be no effort
in wanting to play. Pitches are green all over, and even if it
rains there is some warmth in the air. The problems you can
encounter during summer football are limited, but because it is
early season you can struggle for fitness. That may sound strange.
Surely you are raring to go again? Well, however keen you are and
however much you have worked hard in pre-season training,
there is no substitute for 'match fitness'. It is entirely different from

117

training sessions, five-a-sides and the rest of the fitness schedules. The layoff may only have been four to six weeks, but you still have to readjust to real match conditions, twisting, turning, and of course the physical challenge.

The lush grass takes it toll as well. Groundsmen like to protect their pitches as long as possible, and as a result they cut the grass a fraction long. When this is the case, try to avoid wearing boots with rubber moulded studs. They are not adequate, and if there is any dew on the ground, grip will be affected. A *long stud* is best suited for early-season grassy pitches and only if they're cropped very short and the ground is hard should rubbers be worn.

Diving on summer pitches is a pleasure compared to the end-of-season goalmouths which are bare and devoid of any protection. One of the few problems 'keepers have to contend with during this season is *grass burns*. They don't come from diving to either side but when a 'keeper has to slide out at feet or the like. Vaseline applied to hips and knees helps prevent bad burns.

The bounce of the ball is as predictable as you will get it all season. It doesn't mean you can afford to be sloppy but rarely will there be the unkind bounce off a patch of mud or divot. If the early-season pitch is wet, the only difficulty is judging pace off the turf. Concentration and technique need to be a little sharper than normal, and you need to anticipate the possibilities before the game even begins.

One final point about early-season pitches. If the grass is fractionally too long, be aware that a rolling ball will hold up and make defenders aware that back passes need to be struck firmly.

Autumn

Pitches remain in good condition but goalmouths are losing grass quickly. The climate is so variable at this time of year that you should be prepared for every possibility. If you can, carry rubber moulded and normal-studded boots at all times and make sure your cap and gloves are in good condition. The sun is generally high during the early-season games, but as autumn arrives you will find times when it is sinking fast. Caps need a good peak and sun shades can be particularly helpful.

Where the goalmouths are bare, apply plenty of grease to knees, hips and elbows, and if there is no give in the ground, don't hesitate to wear rubber moulded boots.

Winter

The first advice I would give is to wear an undershirt. In the summer I was happy to wear just a goalkeeping jersey, but if you are to remain supple and mobile there must be plenty of warmth in the body and an undershirt is essential. Pitches can be even more variable during the winter than at any other time of the year, so all types and varieties of equipment should be at hand. These should include long, medium-length and rubber moulded studs and any special boots you may possess for icy pitches.

Goalmouths have generally 'gone' completely by now and in successive games you could be facing:

Firm conditions In effect this means a rolled and compacted mixture of mud and soil. It usually has 'give' in it and a good stud is advisable. There can be unpredictable bounces but not as bad as with muddy conditions.

Mudheaps Constant rain turns the bare goalmouth into a mudbath. To release some of the lying water, goalmouths are spiked and forked, but within minutes of playing on them, they become churned up and quickly take on the look of a ploughed field.

Balls can stick, skid, pick up pace, bounce erratically. You name it, anything goes. Obviously you need to be alert and aware but never fear the possibilities. Even the most hardened observer is more sympathetic to errors in these conditions. In a way you have a built-in excuse, which you should turn to your advantage by taking more of a risk than when good conditions prevail. The same principle applies when you are faced with icy conditions and snow.

Ice and snow If you feel comfortable with kneepads and/or armpads, wear them. Personally I found them uncomfortable and restricting in movement, so I wore a tracksuit bottom with the leg section tucked into socks. Again the choice of tracksuit bottom is personal, but don't wear it too close-fitting. It can prevent or restrict movement, and when stretching a long way will rip in any

The author strives to see what's happening at the other end of the pitch during a heavy snowstorm. *Photo: Peter Jay.*

case. If you are like me, and feel the cold, then make sure you cover as much of the body as possible.

In my opinion, the rocky icy pitches are the most difficult for the 'keeper. Footwork is extremely difficult and needs to be adapted slightly from the normal. Instead of a comfortable stride, steps must be of a smaller, quicker nature – 'little mincers', as when travelling backwards to catch or tip over high balls.

Courage above and beyond the normal is called for in these conditions. After games, bruises and knocks can seem to cover the entire body. There is nothing you can do about it and it's no good looking for sympathy. No one can feel them but you.

Kicking a dead ball can be particularly difficult, so have a word with defenders on two counts – to help you play as many short goal kicks as possible by providing support, and to be alert should you lose your footing and miskick.

All goals are a result of mistakes but in icy, snowy conditions there is even greater likelihood of them happening. Teamwork, support and covering needs to be spot-on, and silly abuse and shouting should be avoided completely. A confident, positive approach is the only answer.

Spring

At this time of year pitches can resemble those in countries like Malta and Cyprus all the year round. Devoid of a blade of grass, rock-hard, bumpy, uninviting. You wake up on match days hoping it's raining, or has been raining, so that there will at least be some 'give' in the ground, and that the bone-shaking saves can wait for another day.

If a pitch is desperately hard and bare, don't be afraid to wear a tracksuit bottom again. Grease all the vulnerable areas of the body. The same type of problems apply as with the other seasons. Rock-hard, and the ball can bounce anywhere. Muddy, and it will zip off the ground and pick up pace. Never assume a shot is easy.

Rubber moulded boots will take a fair old beating towards the end of the season, but always put yourself in a position to change to normal studs at half-time should the weather change during the first forty-five minutes.

Gloves

I have refrained from mentioning the use of gloves on purpose until now. It is an area of goalkeeping which changed drastically between 1970 and 1980. Before then the choice of gloves for 'keepers was limited. There were a few cotton gloves with rubber strips available, but easily the most popular were the thin cotton gloves which could be seen being worn by the majority of leading 'keepers. Even then they were only used when it was wet and the ball greasy and slippy. If it was a dry pitch and a dry day, there would be no possibility of 'keepers using anything other than bare hands.

The 1970 World Cup in Mexico included several 'keepers with an assortment of gloves, and even Gordon Banks of England could be seen trying out an unusual type of glove on a couple of occasions.

After that the gloves market took off in a major way, and by the end of the decade there was a sophisticated range.

There was a time when the 'old school' 'keeper like myself laughed at some of the gloves. I admit to likening Sepp Maier's gloves to a wicketkeeper's in the game of cricket. However, the catching of the West German international over a period of time became so spectacular that to ignore the gloves would have been dangerous. Suddenly the gloves market became flooded, and the old reliable gloves bearing the names of Springett, Banks and Bonetti were competing against others with names like Maier, Curkovic, Hellstroem and Zoff on them. Shilton, Clemence and Parkes in England were quick to put their names to another assortment.

The reason I'm dealing with the history of goalkeepers' gloves is that at the end of the day it is what is inside them and what is inside the player that matters most, not the gloves.

I am not condemning them by any means. Some are little short of sensational in their quality and adhesive powers. Whatever you do, though, don't swap and change constantly. Experiment by all means, but be quite clear in your own mind which pair you feel happiest with. If a particular pair help improve your confidence, stick by them loyally.

You also need to be absolutely certain which conditions are unsuitable for any type of glove. I still feel the thin, close-fitting cotton glove is safest in wet conditions, while some of the rubber-faced gloves are quite extraordinary in dry weather. There is also little doubt that for punching purposes a good pair of gloves will help gain distance, always assuming that the 'keeper's timing is good.

One warning: forearms, wrists, palm of hands and fingers need to be very strong. Wear gloves all the time and hands will definitely *soften*. So make sure that there are training spells or exercises where bare hands are used. Hands are the most important part of a 'keeper's armoury, and I repeat that in the long run it is those hands allied with all the other essential goalkeeping techniques which are important, not a pair of gloves.

Gloves, cap, snow, rain, sleet, ice, mud – all are an integral part of goalkeeping. If the weather is bad and your coach is protecting you from it by training inside, complain. Insist you keep practising in every conceivable weather situation, even if it's only for ten or fifteen minutes. When you take your place in goal, there must be nothing strange or foreign to you. If doubts creep in, they in turn lead to anxiety and error.

There is one weather condition which I have left until last, because it can be found in summer, autumn, winter and spring. A strong *wind* is desperately difficult to contend with. The reason is its unpredictability. The wind comes and goes, gusting one moment, dropping the next. It can affect even well-struck shots, but it is on high crosses and lofted balls into the area that most trouble occurs.

Any dogmatic advice would be stupid. You can read every situation differently and as long as an early decision is made you will always give yourself a chance of going a yard or two further for the ball that is taken away from you, or back-pedalling for the ball that rises more than anticipated.

Looking back at this chapter, it is not one that would exactly inspire anyone to take up goalkeeping. More than likely it would have the opposite effect. It is nonetheless important if we are to acquire an overall awareness of the varied facets of the glory position, and become familiar with them through practice and experiment.

You never stop learning and acquiring knowledge when you play in goal, but if and when weather conditions change dramatically just before kick-off and sunshine turns into sleet, rain and muddy pitch, at least you can adapt without too much concern, fear or tension.

7

'Fitness?
Goalkeepers don't need to be fit!'

One of the greatest fallacies in football is the one that presumes that goalkeepers are nothing like as fit as outfield players. In my experience, professional 'keepers not only join in all the normal running activities and everyday fitness activities, but also spend hours doing their own thing later on.

The best formula is to ensure that the 'keeper joins in some general team fitness training but concentrates on regular, if not daily, specialist work. This is a short chapter which outlines the need for all-round general fitness.

Fitness involves a physical and mental preparedness. All the love for the game and natural skills imaginable count for little if the body and mind have not been tuned for all eventualities. The aim is to use one's skill and knowledge confidently and consistently. If a player falls short and fades in a game it is almost certainly because he is not fit enough.

The unfit goalkeeper is one who:

makes errors of judgement;

loses concentration;

loses technical knowhow.

The fitter goalkeepers are, the more likely they are to cope with all the physical and mental examinations that occur.

All the *bodily contact situations* in 'keeping take their toll. So too does diving, landing, and picking oneself up off the ground. If you are fit you hardly notice collisions. They can be shrugged off easily. But when fitness falls, an average challenge will become a problem.

The stop-start movements involved in keeping goal can all be punishing – short sprints, back-pedalling, twisting, turning and bending all tax your *general mobility*.

Because we are all different it is almost impossible to measure the fatigue caused by *tension and concentration*. You may remember my little story earlier about climbing in the bath at the Arsenal in a shattered state even though I had little work to do. That was purely mental fatigue from having to be alert for every ball, waiting for shots that often didn't occur. Another player badly affected was Charlie George, who scored Arsenal's winner in the 1971 FA Cup final, who was physically sick before almost every game. As I said, individuals differ, but you would be astonished at how many top footballers put on an act in order to hide their nerves and tension.

Fitness helps overcome these three types of fatigue or at least delays them for as long as possible.

Physical fitness

Some of my best friends remain lads I met at Loughborough College between 1960 and 1963. Best friends do tend to disagree a lot though, especially my athlete friends who trained so hard and scoffed openly at the apparently easy schedules undertaken by footballers like myself.

What they failed to understand was that apart from hurdling and steeplechasing all their track events were straight, uninterrupted and unchallenged. Perhaps an occasional jostling and elbowing would occur in middle-distance events. On the other hand footballers and especially goalkeepers are continually interrupted, stopping, starting, tackling, challenging, diving, hitting the ground and generally sustaining all types of blows to fitness, physical and mental. There can be no real argument about it, and it's the reason why the killer events in athletics are those containing barriers to interrupt the flow.

Fitness for any sport becomes a conditioned fitness, and whereas the athlete's interval running and the like would have been of little use to me, mobility exercises, agility training, running up slopes on beaches, playing squash or tennis and the occasional cross country all helped me gain overall fitness for goalkeeping.

Within my fitness training, I was striving particularly for:
STRENGTH – which would represent power and greater SPEED.
MOBILITY – in the form of suppleness. The wider the range of move-

ment within joints and muscles, the greater the sharpness and goalkeeping options there are likely to be.

STAMINA AND ENDURANCE – the two previous areas are only of any great value if they can be sustained for ninety minutes. The exercises to improve stamina and endurance are endless, and there are numerous booklets on the subject. The goalkeeping coaching and training section that follows includes some examples, in particular the pressure exercises.

Weight training is also valuable, because most movements are of an explosive nature, very similar to those encountered in a game. Weights need to be supervised, and a course that suits you must be found. Do too much and there will be dangers of injury or adding unnecessary bulk. Development must be gradual and of a short sharp nature. All the time you are aiming to increase endurance and delay the outset of fatigue. Once fatigue occurs, concentration will waver and confidence will nosedive.

Try to balance a training programme so that no one area is vastly superior to another.

Relate it as much as possible to your needs within a game.

Occasionally extend yourself beyond reasonable limits – a real overload.

Keep a careful check on progress.

Make as many areas of training as possible competitive. It's good for you and always gets a little more effort.

Avoid boredom by regular changes. If you do the same thing continually you will have problems when faced by a new situation. The brain needs to be exercised as much as the body.

Mental fitness

Every running, jumping, twisting and turning exercise imaginable is valuable to delay the outset of fatigue, but when the work load and pressure have got to a certain point, only one thing will save you from losing form and concentration – the mind.

Mental fitness to me means having:

A love affair with the game, unfailing interest and total *enthusiasm.* When it exists, training, travelling, cleaning boots or kit are all enjoyable and never a chore. There is no doubt Kevin Keegan's enthusiasm took him to the top, not just the talents he was born with. Real enthusiasm can be infectious. If others around you see you trying your best, enjoying every moment, they will respond as well.

The will to win. There is little chance of being competitive at anything unless you have a will to succeed. Defeat should never be accepted until the final whistle. Pain must be hidden, determination always obvious.

Confidence. It has already been mentioned many times but again, in the context of mental fitness it is a vital aspect. If you do not possess overall confidence in yourself, in your ability to do things, you are unlikely to succeed.

You must be capable of taking a chance doing your own thing, knowing that you will get 'stick' when you fail. If you never try you will never succeed. A good combination of physical and mental fitness makes all things possible. Things will be attempted without a moment's hesitation, and there is no fear of being let down in the vital last fifteen minutes of a game.

8

The coaching and training of goalkeepers

Try to picture the scene, a football training pitch exposed to the elements. It's cold, pouring with rain and the goalmouths are deep in mud. On such occasions, the incentive to coach or train would seem non-existent. Wembley Stadium appears to be a million miles away.

Simply training for training's sake, though, serves little or no purpose. There must be, at all times, *enthusiasm, enjoyment* and *satisfaction* – for the 'keeper or 'keepers and any other servers or helpers. On top of that, all parties need to show *imagination.* When the 'keeper is included in general fitness work, imagination is not normally required, but when he is doing his own thing, that is working at and improving his goalkeeping, the importance of imagination is paramount. That cold, exposed, muddy goalmouth I mentioned should become Wembley Stadium with a 100,000 crowd watching your every save, every mistake.

This chapter will show how closely related goalkeeping training should be to a match situation. Much of it will be in note form, showing the setting up of an exercise, outlining the purpose of it and finally pointing out the main coaching areas to be developed within it. The practices and exercises included in this chapter are simply a cross-section of the type of activity goalkeepers require. They need to be used sensibly, and varied regularly. You can add other ideas to them as long as the finished exercise bears a strong resemblance to the game situation.

I have to warn that the relationship between the goalkeeping coach and his charge can be delicate, unless, that is, the coach actually played in goal himself. The reason is that all 'keepers soon learn to appreciate just how much of a specialist role they have chosen. Experience alone teaches them the intricate problems that occur. Consequently they do not take easily any heavy criticism by the coach of their positional play or similar goalkeeping difficulties, if that individual has never actually faced the problem personally. When the coach is a former 'keeper, the atmosphere is altogether different. There is immediate respect, a common bond, and frankly it's a case of sharing the same wavelength.

The area of coaching which annoys 'keepers more than any other is 'pressure' training. 'Keepers appreciate of course that there is a place for 'pressure' work because in a game there are moments when a shot on target is blocked and preparation has to be made immediately for a follow-up shot. All the same, *the bulk of goalkeeping training MUST be done sensibly and realistically.* In a real game a goalkeeper does not dive to save, throw the ball to the side and rush into position to face a second shot immediately. This form of training breeds terrible habits, like *bad handling, sloppiness* and *lack of thought*. It does nothing for the 'keeper except improve his reactions slightly and show how much will power or sheer guts he possesses.

Improving a goalkeeper's technique or simply maintaining his standard demands continual association with a match situation. That means a realistic starting position for the 'keeper at every exercise. If he should kill a shot completely, he is given time to release the ball and prepare himself for the next assault. When a shot is parried but stays reasonably close, the 'keeper must obviously chase it. If the parry knocks the ball well away, the coach or helpers will seize on it and try and score in exactly the same manner as in a game.

If a goalkeeper simply goes through the motions of training without thought or enthusiasm the coach has failed totally. It is the responsibility of the coach therefore to ensure that *realism* exists in virtually every training session for goalkeepers.

The warm-up

The warm-up session should include a wide range of exercises that help mobility and suppleness. For the *shoulder* region these can include a variety of arm-circling and arm-presses.

Hip exercises include trunk-curls and rotation movements, and *leg* exercises can involve different forms of jumping, heel-touching, knee-bending, squat thrusts, etc, etc. All of these simple trunk exercises are effective and well proven.

Warm-up *running* activities should all bear some resemblance to the movements required on a match day:

Short sharp sprints over five to ten yards are called for when a ball is overrun or miscontrolled by an attacker; a through ball is hit; or a ball is deflected and falls loose.

Running backwards at varying speeds normally relates to high balls beyond the far post. Stress the need for short, sharp, mincing steps, and not wide strides.

Sideways movements should be practised in two ways:

1) A high, bouncy, on-the-toes method which is quite acceptable when related to game situations where the ball is wide on the flank, but totally unacceptable if the ball is around the penalty area. Then the 'keeper stands to get caught on the upward bounce by a low snap-shot, so:

2) A low, more prepared style is then practised and adopted. The movement sideways is basically the same but the feet need to stay in contact with the ground almost all the time. When the 'keeper moves to his left with a sideways exercise he needs to 'drag' the trailing foot and vice versa when the movement is to the right.

Another important purpose of the warm-up session, and indeed of preparing for a game, is to *shake the whole system*. I believe that until a 'keeper has actually jarred the body by either diving to the ground or colliding with an opponent, he is not fully awake. So because he can face any type of situation or shot within the opening seconds of a match, it is crucial to get the whole system alive. This applies equally to a morning, afternoon or evening training session. Simple *forward* and *backward rolls*, or 'fun' activities where 'keepers try to catch each other off-balance with a *shoulder-charge*, are useful in this respect.

If there are three or four 'keepers warming up together, keep them in a tight group and have them dodge in and out of each other. You can adapt this exercise for bodily contact practice or simply to develop good footwork.

In this warm-up section I have only touched on some old and some new activities, but before moving on to a variety of goalkeeping practices, I would like to stress the *importance of a pre-match warm-up*.

It is not enough when you are a 'keeper to expect to go into a game cold and perform adequately. It is virtually impossible to turn form on and off like a light switch. The pre-match warm-up spell is crucial in order for a 'keeper to prepare himself mentally and physically to do battle. Part of the mental preparation actually comes in fact from putting aside ten minutes for a set routine of exercises. For instance my own warm-up before any match consisted of the following:

Shoulder-presses and exercises, trunk-curls, groin-stretching, hamstring-stretching, ankle-stretching, sit-ups, twelve press-ups, and plenty of handling of a ball by throwing it against a wall or having some person throw it at me. I would then put the first finger of each hand into the corners of my eyes to get out any 'sleepiness', followed up by washing my face in really cold water and finally shaking the system up completely by shoulder-charging the wall six to ten times! All told it took me about fifteen minutes to prepare myself in this manner. My range of activities got me completely warm and, more important, put me in the right frame of mind for the game.

I have to admit that the religious way in which I undertook a warm-up bordered on the superstitious. Superstition isn't a bad thing as long as it helps you psychologically.

So much for the importance of a warm-up period on match days and before training. It's time now to set before you a range of goalkeeping practices which have worked very well for me either during my own playing career or when coaching fellow 'keepers.

Concentration sessions

If you would cast your mind back for a moment to the chapter on personal qualities, you may remember the first quality I listed – the ability to look at yourself. When the game is in progress that ability is needed more than at any other time. You can start a game feeling one hundred per cent fit and happy, and yet play hope-lessly. Similarly you may have had flu and turn up to play feeling well below par, but to your amazement finish up giving a great performance.

My one-, two- or three-minute concentration sessions are aimed at improving one's ability to assess just why things are going wrong and what can be attempted to rectify the situation.

Set-up   Three or four 'keepers ten to fifteen yards apart (see Figure 27) with a good landing surface but not necessarily any goals. There needs to be just one ball, which can be thrown, kicked or volleyed. There must always be three sessions, whether it be for a one-minute, two-minute or three-minute period. In between each session there is a half minute's complete relaxation when the 'keeper literally switches off. It doesn't matter in what order the sessions take place, but they must consist of the fol-lowing:

1) *An intense spell.* In this minute the 'keeper puts on an act and purposefully gets himself charged up. Everything is rushed and over-intense. Catching and diving are carried out as normal, but in a totally false manner compared to the individual's normal style.

2) *A sloppy spell.* This is the complete opposite to the previous activity. Each 'keeper is relaxed, casual, overconfident, even cocky. The art of goalkeeping is too easy for him in this spell. It is the other extreme to the individual's normal style.

3) *Being yourself.* In the third session you handle and stop the ball in completely your own style, as you see yourself. Concentra-

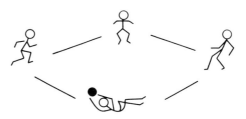

Figure 27

tion is maintained throughout the period the activity takes place, whether it be for one, two or three minutes. Basically you undertake the activity in the style in which you would play a real game.

The purpose of these sessions should be fairly obvious. A 'keeper should formulate in his mind a perfect picture of himself, so that on those days when things go wrong, he can make a quick assessment and decide whether he is a little too intense or too casual and relaxed. If the 'keeper does the concentration exercise often enough he will be able to recognize it and make tiny adjustments to his play.

The exercise can be varied enormously. The minute spells should be used for, say, purely catching the ball away from the body, or dealing with difficult shots bouncing just awkwardly in front of the 'keeper. The distance between the 'keepers can also change. Ten to fifteen yards for the normal exercise, but for reaction saves the distance can be as little as five yards and for distance shots anything up to twenty to twenty-five yards.

One final tip – one minute means one minute, two minutes means two minutes. It is easy to forget time, so don't get carried away with the activity, otherwise it will lose its purpose completely.

Footwork

Most of the exercises in this section need good footwork. Here are several, however, that are designed specifically for that purpose.

Piggy in the middle

A circle is formed of three, four or any number of individuals. Only two footballs are required. The 'keeper is in the centre of the circle. A shot or throw is delivered at or around the 'keeper, who saves and delivers to another member of the circle, before spinning and facing the next ball – see Figure 28 overleaf. As he is under pressure the time in the middle is restricted – thirty seconds to one minute maximum.

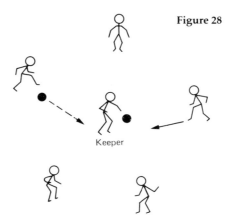

Figure 28

Keeper

Rather have two or three sessions of high quality than one session of poor quality. Those serving must give the 'keeper a chance to save and release before shooting themselves.

COACHING POINTS

1) Short sharp steps at all times.
2) If the circle is quite close, make sure your feet stay in contact with the ground and that you don't get too bouncy.
3) Keep 'switched on' to the possibility of shots being fired at you when you're still moving.
4) Agility, mobility.
5) If a ball is stopped but not held, chase it instantly.

The triangle

In this exercise the 'keeper is defending three goals (see Figure 29) and is in constant action for whatever number of shots the coach thinks fit, up to a maximum of eight. The exercise should be done twice, the first time with the 'keeper moving to the right and the second time moving to the left.

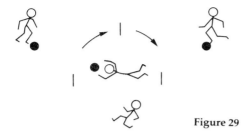

Figure 29

COACHING POINTS

1) Short sharp steps.
2) Be alive to shots that catch you still moving.
3) If you can hold the shot, do so.
4) Servers must give the 'keeper a chance.
5) It is a pressure exercise and exhausting, but it is short and sweet.
6) Determination.
7) Speed of thought – pounce on a half-saved shot.
8) Six to eight balls required.

Move and save

The 'keeper stands on or close to his line facing the server or servers. You can have three to four servers spread around the penalty area or just one who keeps moving to left or right in order to change the 'keeper's angle – see Figure 30. The 'keeper *dictates*

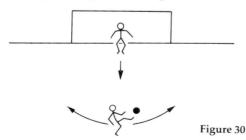

Figure 30

this exercise, which is one designed to sharpen his awareness of the shot which gets fired in before there is time to *set* himself properly. In a game this occurs all the time. It is not an ideal world and a swift pass can be met by a shot which catches the 'keeper still on the move, trying to adjust his angle.

The 'keeper dictates this exercise by a forward movement. As soon as that movement is made the servers can shoot.

COACHING POINTS

1) Be settled every time. No rush whatsoever.
2) Make the movement to face the ball realistic. It must be as you would do it in a game.
3) Try and get some sort of set position as the ball is struck.
4) Complete awareness of possibilities.
5) Saves are fine with any and every part of the body.
6) React instantly to the loose ball – chase it.
7) When any one save is made, take your time going back to the starting position.
NB This exercise can be varied and adapted easily to include several servers, numerous changes of angle. Think of the game and incidents when 'keepers are dragged out of position or pulled forward as a shot is fired at goal.

Turn and face

This is an exercise which contains speed of thought, saving on the move, narrowing the angle. The 'keeper's starting position is on or close to his line facing *into* the net. The servers representing the forwards can be anywhere in and around the edge of the penalty area – see Figure 31. The coach, who can be one of the servers, ensures that the 'keeper has his back turned before pointing to one of the forwards who will be responsible for the shot on the command 'go'. The 'keeper has to spin, pick up the movement of the attacker and attempt to form some sort of angle as the ball is struck.

Clearly the men shooting have to use common sense and give

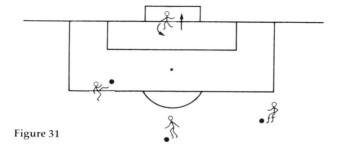

Figure 31

the 'keeper some reasonable chance. The shots can be fired at goal in any manner whatsoever and from any distance. In other words, vary it continually so that the 'keeper on the word 'go' turns to find a shot coming from twenty yards or as close as six yards.

COACHING POINTS

1) Fast spin but controlled footwork.
2) Composure.
3) Stay in contact with the ground.
4) Try and pick up the movement of the attacker as quickly as possible.
5) Steady head. Any sharp jerky movement and you won't be able to focus.
6) Stay in contact with the ground or you could get caught off-balance.
7) Awareness. It is similar to the previous 'move and save' exercise, but with angling involved.
8) Razor-sharp reactions, in case the shot is from five to six yards away.
9) Chase any loose balls.
10) No rush involved whatsoever in the practising of the exercise.
11) Any rebounds should be finished by alert servers.
12) Balls required – ideally twelve, minimum six.

No-hope ally

You will remember in the chapter on techniques that I indicated the low cross from near the sideline was desperately difficult because of the numerous alternatives that were presented. These include:

  a shot inside the near post,
  a low cross within reach,
  a sharp near-post pull-back,
  a mid-goal pull-back,
  a far-post chip.

Just to name five!

  I call it 'no-hope ally' because if the ball is not at or around the 'keeper, he looks to all intents and purposes hopelessly beaten. As I've been pointing out, though, in goalkeeping you are never beaten. You must never surrender. When the pull-back reaches the forward, it's possible that he may relax and side-foot the ball casually, or rush his shot and miscue. A variety of things can happen, so the 'keeper must never give up. Admittedly the odds can be stacked against him, but two saves out of five is a distinct possibility, as long as his mind is attuned to the possibilities.

Set-up   A pile of footballs should be placed near the edge of the penalty area, out wide. The 'keeper starts at the near post as he would if the attacker was near the goal-line just inside the box. The attacker/server varies his service from the goal-line to include the full range of cross previously discussed, and that includes a shot at the 'keeper or inside the near post. See Figure 32.

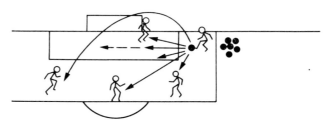

Figure 32

COACHING POINTS

1)   Beware the shot inside the near post.
2)   Only go for the low cross if you really think you can get it.
3)   Go, and then miss it, and you have no chance. So at least buy yourself a second chance if in doubt.
4)   Stay in a low stance, ready to pounce or spin.
5)   For the near-post pull-back, any save is likely to be instinctive and chancy.
6)   When the pull-back finds an attacker in mid-goal, you can spin and perhaps get in a couple of small strides.
7)   A ball struck low to the far post will enable you to get two or three steps in before a desperate dive.
8)   A chip to the far post gives you most chance because it allows a second or two longer in which to turn and travel across your goal.
9)   When spinning from the near post, avoid moving in an arc.
10)   The spin should be flat to keep you close to the line and permit desperate last-ditch saves.
11)   Be aware of the body as a barrier.
12)   When taking a chance and diving in the hope of a shot hitting the body, try and make the body as long and as wide as possible, with toes pointed.
13)   If any cross should give you time to get into a good position, resist the temptation to dive aimlessly and early. In this situation you will have a very real chance to react after the ball is on its way to goal.
14)   The server and attackers must have realism in each attempt. Virtually all the coaching points I have outlined in the 'no-hope ally' exercise apply to a very similar alternative practice which I will call:

Even-less-hope ally

This is an even more difficult situation with less time to react. It is not quite as realistic as the first exercise, but practised over a period of time it improves a 'keeper's reaction to any seemingly hopeless open-goal situation.

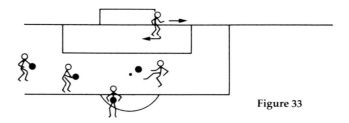

Figure 33

Set-up Six to eight balls minimum and one or several servers. The 'keeper stands by his near post facing the corner flag. A server or several servers stand in and around the penalty area with a ball each – see Figure 33. The coach points to one of the players holding a ball and on the command of 'go' the 'keeper spins and attempts to keep out any shot directed at goal. Naturally some common sense has to be used by the attackers, but basically they can volley, half-volley, drive or swerve any shot goalwards and from any position they wish within the box.

The only *coaching points* I would give in addition to the earlier practice is to ensure that the 'keepers get regular 'joy'. This is easily done by firing the occasional shot directly at them.

Checking positional play and angles

There are plenty of ways of checking whether 'keepers are positioning themselves well. The *spin and turn* exercise already mentioned is one, but it is unnatural in that the 'keeper starts with his back to play. The easiest practice involves the coach moving at random around the penalty area with a ball and continually stopping, feinting to shoot and even occasionally trying to exploit any gap the 'keeper has left. See Figure 34.

COACHING POINTS

1)   Stay low and prepared all the time.
2)   Be prepared for a shot all the time.

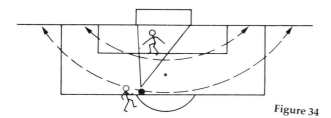

Figure 34

3)   Footwork has to be short and sharp.
4)   Make yourself as big as possible.
5)   Have identifying marks so that you can check the angle continually.
6)   Think of a double arc which surrounds the goal (dotted lines) – one which you move around and one which the coach with the ball moves around. They are not rigid lines, just imaginary ones which exist all the time and at whatever distance the ball is from goal.
NB One or several people can be involved to test the 'keeper.

Pass and shoot or catch and throw

This is a variation on the last exercise. Three or four players move around the penalty area either playing the ball on the ground with feet or throwing it to each other. Movement must be realistic and at any time one of the players can shoot (or throw) the ball at goal. The 'keeper has to keep adjusting his position and angle all the time, as well as being aware that a shot (or throw) is imminent. See Figure 35.

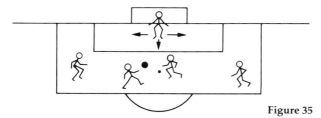

Figure 35

Deflections

Throughout the book I have indicated that there is no such thing as a certainty when keeping goal. There are a wide variety of reasons why the position is one of total unpredictability. Conditions, mishit, swerving or dipping shots and the like demand intense concentration by the 'keeper, an alertness that enables him to react instinctively in any emergency. The biggest *emergency* of all is when a goal-bound shot hits another player (i.e. opponent or colleague) and is deflected to a different part of the goal from that to which the 'keeper is going.

The following two exercises are excellent for improving awareness and reaction saves. I will outline both before listing the coaching points, which are the same for each activity.

Exercise 1

Set-up Minimum of six to eight balls; minimum of two assistants and maximum four to five. The 'keeper stands near his goal-line. One individual stands on or around the six-yard line. The rest have a ball each and in turn, and *only* when the 'keeper is set each time, fire the ball *straight at* the man on the six-yard line. He in turn *deflects* the shot with any part of the body including hands. The deflection can be *gentle* – a very faint touch – or *heavy* – a strong touch. See Figure 36.

Don't worry about the odd service being wide of the man deflecting. It helps to give the 'keeper some joy, and ensures that

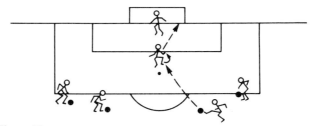

Figure 36

he will always be attacking the original shot, even though he is aware a deflection may occur. Shots at the goal can be either off the floor or from the server's hand.

Exercise 2

Set-up Minimum of six to eight balls; one or several assistants; six to eight cones. In this exercise the shots at goal are kept low, so that they *might* hit one of the cones and take a deflection or might miss them and continue on a straight path. As with Exercise 1, the 'keeper must go for the original shot while being aware that a deflection is on. The *concentration* involved is incredible, so remember the exercise can be used solely for that purpose as well as deflections. See Figure 37.

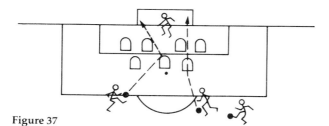

Figure 37

COACHING POINTS

1) Supreme concentration at all times.
2) *Always* read the first angle of the shot.
3) *Never* anticipate a deflection because should it not occur, it may be too late.
4) Only *be aware* that a deflection can occur any time.
5) Awareness of all parts of the body, so that a foot or arm can suddenly be thrown in a different direction should a deflection occur.
6) Chase immediately any half-saved effort.

7)   There will be blind spots occasionally when a ball crosses in front of a cone.

8)   Servers vary pace and type of shot and occasionally place shots wide of the six-yard man (Exercise 1) or over the cones (Exercise 2) for a straightforward save. Use imagination at all times.

Crosses

It is not easy to get realism into the coaching of high crosses without running the risk of injury to both the 'keeper and the player challenging him on the cross. High crosses and punching are dangerous contact areas at all times, so be warned. I would suggest three ways of coaching 'keepers to catch high crosses.

Exercise 1

Set-up Minimum of six balls; one goalmouth; one or several servers. The goalkeeper stands within his goal and faces a variety of cross from either wing – see Figure 38. He is unchallenged at all times. The service can be:

from the ground striking a moving ball;

thrown from hand, which may appear unrealistic but is a good way of ensuring accuracy;

a set piece, i.e. a corner or free kick situation.

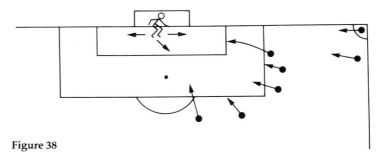

Figure 38

COACHING POINTS

1) Goalkeeper adjusts position according to where the ball is hit from. (NB Remember the basic rule! The closer to goal the ball is hit, the more the 'keeper is dragged to the near post and vice versa.)

2) You can be as bouncy as you like in goal for a cross hit from the flank.

3) Lose a little bounce if the ball is struck from the edge of the penalty area.

4) Make the decision to go or stay confidently and quickly.

5) You should be able to pick up the flight of the ball within four or five yards of the cross being struck.

6) Attack the ball, be positive.

7) Collect the ball at the highest point possible from a powerful spring.

8) Pull the ball into your chest as quickly as possible.

9) Stay compact.

10) Be strong.

11) Go to ground when off-balance.

Exercise 2

Exactly the same as Exercise 1 but with someone *challenging* the 'keeper on the cross – see Figure 39. All the points stressed in the first exercise apply and the only addition concerns the *decision to punch or catch*. This must again be made quickly and confidently and if the choice is a *punch*, all the points of technique need to be applied – short, sharp punch, as big a contact area as possible, etc.

Figure 39

Exercise 3

In Exercise 3 all the same coaching points apply, but the exercise involves packing the goalmouth with as many people as possible, and ideally a minimum of six bodies – see Figure 40. The crosses are varied as before. The 'keeper's choice of decision remains the same, i.e. to catch or punch. The 'bodies' in the box can challenge but, as in Exercise 2, need to be told to *use some common sense* in the manner they challenge.

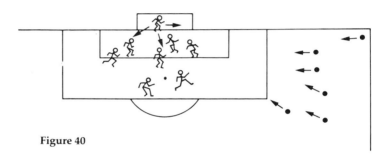

Figure 40

Specialized punching exercise

The exercise I am about to outline is invaluable and I can guarantee that it has beneficial effects in the long term. The reason I am so emphatic about it is that it improved my technique enormously. Orginally I was a poor puncher of the ball. I wanted to catch every time. Unfortunately the higher the level you play the more you appreciate that a punch is at times essential. Regular practice of this punching exercise develops excellent long-term results. Punching, remember, is a last-ditch technique. It involves a 'keeper lunging over the top of an offending body or bodies.

Set-up   The 'keeper lies flat on the ground on his stomach facing the coach four to five yards away. The coach has several balls available to him, should any punch be misdirected and not come back to him – see Figure 41. The ground represents an opponent

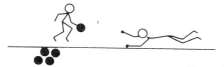

Figure 41

backing into the 'keeper. His awkward position lying on his tummy is very similar to the one he faces when trying to punch. The ball is delivered approximately two to three feet off the ground at the prone 'keeper. The 'keeper attempts to punch the ball straight back at the server.

The exercise should consist of between six and twelve punches, which can be *double-fisted* or *single-fisted*. When practising a double-handed punch the 'keeper's body position is flat. When the single-fisted punch is practised, the body should be slightly inclined one way or the other, depending on whether the left or right hand is being used to punch.

COACHING POINTS

1) Concentration.
2) Suppleness in the small of the back.
3) Timing most important.
4) The punch should travel four to six inches for accuracy and consistency.
5) Develop power.
6) Try and knock the coach over with the punch.
7) Be aggressive.
8) I would recommend twelve double-fisted punches followed by a short break, followed by twelve right-handed punches, followed by a short break, followed by twelve left-handed punches.
NB To the coach! Bully the 'keeper. Tell him he's soft and that there's not enough power in the punch. Encourage the 'keeper ot be a bit angry without losing his timing.

Courage and diving at feet

How do you coach courage? Surely courage is inborn. Well, to an extent this is true but you can also sharpen, improve and even develop a 'keeper's courage with the following two exercises.

Grid work

If a marked grid area is not available, set up an area about ten yards square. The 'keeper is opposed in the square by one, two or three opponents who try to keep possession between them – see Figure 42. The objective of the 'keeper is to either win the ball off the opposition or deflect it outside the square by any legal means, but basically by diving at feet. It is a very demanding exercise mentally and physically, so build it up gradually. To begin with, get the 'keeper to 'win' three balls only. As the 'keeper becomes more proficient, build the exercise up until he is asked to win eight balls from the opponents.

If numbers aren't available, the exercise is still worthwhile on a one-to-one basis.

Figure 42

COACHING POINTS

1)   Stay low.
2)   Don't dive in rashly.
3)   Be composed.
4)   Try to threaten the man on the ball physically.

5)   Look for any miscontrol or hesitation.
6)   Be confident.
7)   Try to force the opponent into error by an occasional feint.
8)   Attack the loose ball instinctively and without fear.
9)   Be aware that a pass might be made at any time.
10)   Watch for the man on the ball trying to attempt a dribble.
11)   If the coach/opponent puts his body between you and the ball, BEWARE –related to a game it means any foul by you would be a PENALTY.
12)   Body awareness, save by feet, knee, arm, leg, hand, etc.
13)   Be positive, strong and determined.
14)   There is no room for fear.
NB to coach. If the 'keeper wins the ball cleanly, it is still worthwhile falling on top of him and even attempting to wrestle the ball away from his grasp. This develops strength and determination on the 'keeper's part.

Virtually all these coaching points can be applied to the second exercise for courage.

One versus one

In this exercise a proper goalmouth is required. One or more outfield players run at goal in turn from twenty-five yards, with a ball at their feet, and attempt to score – see Figure 43 overleaf. The 'keeper uses all his initiative, knowledge and courage to prevent a goal.

COACHING POINTS

The same points apply as in *grid work*, but with a few additions and modifications.
1)   Make every attack realistic. The 'keeper should not be asked to save one goal attempt and then be rushed into facing another.
2)   The exercise requires time and as realistic a match situation as is possible.
3)   Vary the angle of the approach.
4)   The attackers can attempt to *dribble* round the 'keeper, *shoot* past the 'keeper, or *chip* the 'keeper.

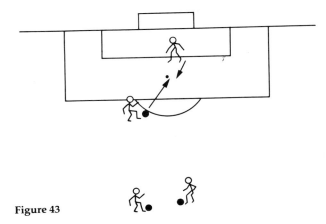

Figure 43

5)   The 'keeper has to call on all the technique points outlined in Chapter 4.
6)   This exercise clearly embraces and develops a 'keeper's ability to narrow the angle as well as developing courage.

Reaction saves

There are a multitude of practices to sharpen a 'keeper's reactions. Even the *triangle* and *turn and face* exercises already outlined can be included in this category, but it's a case of using your head and varying the practices. So here are just a few more examples, most of which are very adaptable.

Sitting

This is one of the best goalkeeping exercises available. I am placing it in the reaction section but it is also good for basic handling, developing suppleness, building up the stomach muscles and moving the body weight.

  The 'keeper sits facing the coach, who throws the ball in turn to

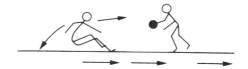

Figure 44

the left and right at a rapid pace – see Figure 44. Not only must the 'keeper catch the ball each time while twisting and stretching one way or the other, he must also move his whole body forward each time the ball is returned. This is done by a little shuffle involving feet and bottom. The number of catches depends on the individual 'keeper's ability, but normally I ask my professional charges to do two sessions of twenty-five.

The exercise demands from the 'keeper determination, agility, concentration, composure, good handling, strength and stamina. It's an exercise which can be developed and varied so that the 'keeper starts *sitting* and catching, moves on to *kneeling* and catching, then *squatting* and catching and finally *standing upright* and catching.

Spin and face

In the starting position the 'keeper has his back to the coach. On the command 'go' the 'keeper spins and attempts to save the ball which is thrown or kicked by the coach – see Figure 45. The throw or kick can be placed anywhere and at a variety of speeds. Often the save will be a sheer reflex effort, with the 'keeper only picking up sight of the ball when it is upon him.

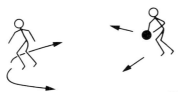

Figure 45

Continuous barrage

Set-up Two servers with six balls each. The exercise is a demanding one but lasts no more than twenty to thirty seconds. A ball is
thrown or kicked by the servers in turn and the 'keeper has to keep
the shots out by any means at his disposal – see Figure 46. The
shots must always give the 'keeper a chance to save. It is a purely
reflex pressure session and the 'keeper does not have to chase a
loose ball if he has parried it.

The coach needs to encourage the 'keeper greatly for although
the duration of the exercise is short, it is nonetheless an exhausting activity. Determination, composure, agility and mobility are
vital if the 'keeper is to do the exercise well.

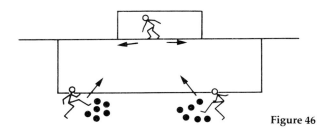

Figure 46

Corrigan session

I have named this next exercise after the Manchester City and
England 'keeper Joe Corrigan, simply because he did it better than
anyone else I've ever seen. It is not only a session to sharpen
reactions, but also one from which you can learn a great deal about
the enthusiasm and determination of any 'keeper.

Set-up Twelve balls are required. Six are placed on the six-yard
line facing the 'keeper's right-hand post. The other six are on the
six-yard line opposite the 'keeper's left-hand post. The servers
have to give the 'keeper a chance again with their throws, half of
which should be directed to the bottom corner and the other half
to the top corner. See Figure 47.

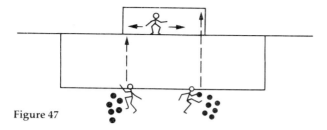

Figure 47

So the 'keeper is plunging low to six balls and soaring high for the other six. It is a 'killer' exercise and needs to be the penulti-mate activity in any session. As the 'keeper gets conditioned to the exercise, he can repeat it after a two- to three-minute rest. On the second session he plunges and soars the opposite way to the first session.

The coach needs to *scream* encouragement at the 'keeper and to praise continually.

Moving body weight

There are often times when a 'keeper dives to a shot which never arrives because it gets blocked. Consequently he is then asked to lift his body weight quickly to face any follow-up. The previous two exercises develop the ability to lift the body weight quickly, and here's a third.

The coach stands four to six yards from the 'keeper, who in turn is lying sideways on the ground facing to the left. The coach then serves the ball so that the 'keeper can dive and catch – see Figure 48.

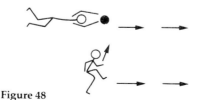

Figure 48

As soon as the ball is returned by the 'keeper the coach repeats the movement. How many saves are made depends on the ability of the 'keeper, but eight to the left followed immediately by eight to the right should be enough.

Team shooting

Apart from specialized work the 'keeper benefits from team shooting practice. Shooting sessions should be varied to include all types of close saves and distance saves. Here's just one example which calls for all-round expertise and knowledge by the 'keeper. The attacker 'a' lays a ball up to a target man 'b' who plays the ball right or left for 'a' to shoot at goal – see Figure 49. The 'keeper covers a wide variety of techniques in saving, i.e. all sorts of diving saves, catching, positional play, narrowing the angle, etc.

The coach decides whether the exercise is done under *pressure*, demanding constant movement by the 'keeper, or in *match situation*, where the 'keeper has time to recover and re-position between each shot.

Long distance

Once upon a time any 'keeper who let in a shot from outside the eighteen-yard line was openly condemned. Times have changed.

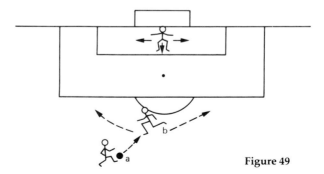

Figure 49

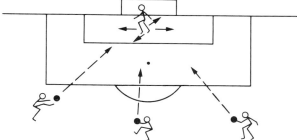

Figure 50

Now it's commonplace to see a goal scored from distance. That's mainly because there is less pressure in the footballs now, enabling them to fly, dip and swerve more often. So 'keepers need to experience all these difficulties regularly in training and can do so with this one excellent activity.

Set-up A minimum of eight balls are required. Ideally there should be three or four servers. A proper goalmouth is required for this exercise, which simply involves the servers hitting shots at goal from anything between eighteen and thirty yards – see Figure 50. It is best if the shots are struck from the hand for both accuracy and variety. The shots should consist of a variety of half-volleys, full volleys, sliced, curled, dipped or driven.

The exercise is never rushed. The 'keeper always has time to readjust after saving, before saving the next shot.

COACHING POINTS

1) Try to cut the angle down before the shot is struck.
2) Don't get caught on an upward bounce.
3) Pick up any dip, slice or swerve early.
4) Good footwork is required, usually of a short, sharp nature.
5) Never assume anything.
6) The ball is not dead until it is in your arms, out of play or in the back of the net!
7) Follow every shot that is off target until it is out of play.
8) Vicious swerving, dipping or bouncing shots may be stopped but not held. So be prepared to chase the loose ball.

I have tried to outline a variety of goalkeeping exercises, all of which can be related to a full match situation. The range and choice of activity is endless. So all I would advise once again is that you use your imagination, whether you are the coach or the 'keeper. Watch games carefully and think up training activities that reproduce a similar situation.

The chief objective of specialized goalkeeping training is that the 'keeper experiences every conceivable match situation, and as a result faces a real game free of fear and apprehension. Time should also be set aside regularly for the 'keeper to practise his kicking and throwing, as well as for sessions which involve team organization at all set pieces, including penalties.

The real secret is to find a nice balance in the goalkeeper's training between team involvement and specialist work. Even then 'keepers must be encouraged to practise by themselves. A flat wall can become the 'keeper's greatest friend. Throwing, kicking, catching or bouncing a ball against one builds a 'keeper's self-confidence, and it's a mixture of confidence and consistency which counts at the end of the day.

Throughout my goalkeeping career, which began when I was eight, I spent hours facing a wall. If a friend or one of the family was available I would ask them to serve for me. There's even one practice I use to this day for any 'keepers I coach. The 'keeper stands with his back to the server, who kicks or throws the ball against the wall. It's another super exercise for developing reactions, and the distance the 'keeper stands from the wall can be varied according to ability and the level of success achieved. See Figure 51.

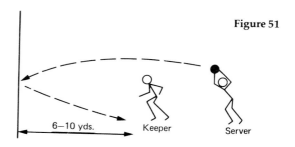

Figure 51

6–10 yds.   Keeper   Server

Competitiveness

Good coaching involves information, encouragement, enthusiasm and competition. Perhaps this chapter has revealed all but the latter aspect, and here again there are numerous ways of developing a competitive spirit.

Basic handling games involving two or more 'keepers are great fun. For instance, in the exercise shown in Figure 52 the 'keepers throw or volley towards each other and have to catch cleanly. Two fumbled saves and they drop out. It's a game which also aids concentration.

The activity can be chopped and changed all the time so that the 'keepers have, for example, to:
1)   Cleanly collect a ball which bounces just in front of them.
2)   Catch all throws or shots away from the body.
3)   Catch cleanly while sitting on the floor six yards apart.
4)   Try to catch each other out from close range, i.e. three to four yards apart.
There are lots more highly competitive goalkeeping exercises.

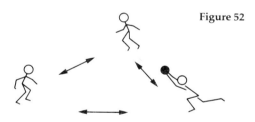

Figure 52

One-versus-one throwing

In this *throwing* activity, two goals should be placed sixteen to eighteen yards apart. The width of the goals should be six yards. The 'keepers then compete against each other and try to score a goal by a good throw. See Figure 53 overleaf.

Figure 53

Two versus two

This is a highly popular game amongst 'keepers. Two full-size goals are placed eighteen yards apart and each goal is protected by two 'keepers. Goals can be scored by a throw or kick but must be struck within two to three yards of the attackers' goal-line. Shots are taken alternately. The coach stands midway between the goals and he acts as referee – see Figure 54. If a ball, on being parried or hitting the woodwork, bounces back over the halfway line away from the defending side, the attacking team have an extra shot.

Take my word for it, the range of saves which occur are nothing short of sensational. The game also develops teamwork and cama-raderie. It can be developed by adding a poaching forward to each side. When throws or shots are delivered the forward stands to the side, but he is able to seize on any fumble or mishandle by the 'keepers and attempt to score a goal for his side.

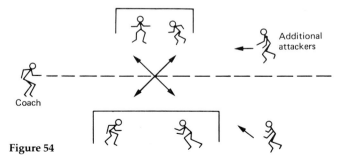

Figure 54

It's right that this chapter on training and coaching should draw to a close with an activity which is so enjoyable, because keeping goal can be a lonely occupation. If things go wrong it is even worse than that – it's a 'rotten' occupation. So enjoyment and satisfaction in training are essential. They restore confidence and mend hurt pride.

Finally, remember that training for goalkeepers can take place anywhere and everywhere – against a brick wall, on grass, in a sandpit, even whilst playing other sports such as squash, badminton, volleyball and basketball.

Who knows? If you have talent and work hard and long enough the image of playing at Wembley in front of a hundred thousand fans could even become reality.

9

Introduction of goalkeeping in primary school

When teams are picked for a game of football at school or in the park, the same old question recurs: 'Who is going in goal?' There are two or three reasons for the reluctance of youngsters under the age of ten to go between the sticks or jackets!

Most kids associate with the goal scorer not the goal stopper. The media are always full of glory stories about goalscoring feats and while the feats of Clemence, Jennings, Shilton, Corrigan and the rest inspire, it's far more difficult emulating a back-breaking death-defying save than getting the ball in the net with a mishit shot or fluke. It's true even at the top level, and a good example was Jimmy Greenhoff's Cup winner for Manchester United against Liverpool in 1977, which he knew little or nothing about, as Lou Macari's shot cannoned off Greenhoff's back to creep in past Ray Clemence.

Apart from the basic difficulties in saving and angling, school-boy games can also tend to get very one-sided and a young 'keeper can have long spells of inactivity. Then there is the fact that no youngster enjoys being on the receiving end of the abuse, and there is plenty of that if you slip up in goal in kickarounds in the playground or park.

The whole question of introducing goalkeeping to a primary school boy is made worse because youngsters of that age usually have boundless energy, and it's difficult to release such enthusiasm in the confined area of a goalmouth.

Anyway, my advice on the introduction of goalkeeping would be exactly the same as it would be for any outfield position. Don't let them choose! Rather ensure that over a period of time all eleven positions and roles within a team are experienced. Only time will indicate 'naturals' in most positions, and it is wrong to assume that a big boy has to be perfect for the central defending position. There are countless examples of top-class players starting their professional careers in one position and finishing up in an entirely different one.

In advocating a wide choice of position for youngsters, I would pay little attention to rigid team formations. By all means start to instil basic techniques by enjoyable activities and practices, but steer clear of 4-2-4, 4-3-3 or 8-1-1 formations and the like. To most youngsters you are causing confusion, and there is plenty of time later to develop set team formations.

Real *enjoyment* of playing football is of paramount importance at primary school level, and the best way of achieving that is by small-sided games, in particular five-a-sides.

The five-a-side game enables everyone to be involved all the time, and the teacher or coach is soon given an insight into who can do what. The great plus of five-a-sides for young goalkeepers is that:

1)   They are constantly in the game, with few dull moments. One hundred per cent concentration is demanded at all times.

2)   They don't suffer from bodily contact or fear of charging. There is a protected area and early knowledge of goalkeeping is confined to shot-stopping and narrowing the angle.

3)   They are in a limited goal as compared to a full-sized one and therefore must stand more chance of saving shots and gaining satisfaction from being the hero. This point is the most important. Obviously a youngster who lets in almost every shot on goal, having waited anxiously for a chance to do his stuff, is going to quickly reject the goalkeeping position.

Small-sided games will soon make it apparent which lads have potential, and with proper encouragement they will retain their interest in goalkeeping until the secondary school stage. A certain amount of discretion must be used in teaching the basic skills of goalkeeping but a boy needs a foundation upon which to build when he arrives at secondary school.

Stage one

At the earliest stage, make any goalkeeping practice a group activity. Simple rolling, catching and throwing practices in fairly stationary positions are sufficient. These activities can be done in groups of two or three or, if you have enough room, even individually against a wall. Gradually there is a progression to moving towards a rolling ball, moving away from it and eventually to diving for the ball which cannot be reached in time to get the body behind it.

In these early stages the only important points of technique to stress are:

1)　Keeping the eye on the ball.

2)　Trying to get some part of the body behind the ball so that if the hands fail to collect, there is still a barrier to prevent the ball from passing.

3)　Keeping the head steady. If a youngster moves his head sharply he will lose good sighting of the ball.

4)　Don't snatch at anything, otherwise it will not stick.

5)　Having strong fingers, hands, wrists and forearms. If wrists and fingers are sloppy any firm shot is likely to get through.

6)　Concentration – don't ever assume any shot is easy, even a back pass. Only when the ball is saved and dead can the 'keeper afford any form of slight relaxation.

Stage two

All those points of technique can be furthered in Stage 2, when each youngster is put under the spotlight for the first time.

A five-a-side goal would be the best size but if not, a normal goal would suffice. All that is required is for shots to come in from a sensible distance – say, around the eighteen-yard line – which would in fact favour the 'keeper, and at a given signal, so that it is not a pressure training session. You should already know what my thoughts are on that matter.

When confidence has built to a point where no youngster dreads making a fool of himself there can be a gradual build-up in a variety of shots. From this point you can start to develop an awareness of angles by having the group form an arc outside the eighteen-yard line and in turn, or at a given signal, move forward and shoot. Again the strike should be from a very stoppable position: the point of the exercise is to get the 'keeper used to moving all round his goalmouth and to improve his awareness of his position in relation to the goal. See Figure 55.

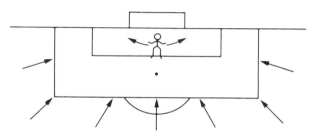

Figure 55

Stage three

Catching the high ball

I have yet to encounter a youngster under ten who has both the confidence and a hand span capable of holding on consistently to a well-struck shot or cross off the ground. In goalkeeping you play the odds all the time, and in this aspect you must assure the primary-school youngster that catching balls cleanly is not easy and at their age not vital either.

What is vital? That their awareness of dropping shots and crosses is such that they are almost tuned to chasing the loose ball even before it's loose – see Figure 56. In other words, they know

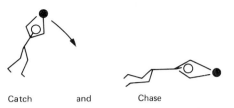

Catch   and   Chase

Figure 56

exactly how to react after their fumble by being quicker to the
cross ball than an opponent. Only practice and more practice at
catching will improve the situation, plus the natural developments
in physique.

Don't worry about punching. A seven- to ten-year-old hasn't
got the strength or coordination to get any distance at punching.
This will come later at secondary school. Other important long-
term goalkeeping areas, such as diving at forwards' feet, can be
explained if a boy is desperate enough to learn, but generally you
should let them develop their own natural techniques at this early
stage and only advise them if they are way off the mark.

Discretion then is the operative word when developing young
goalkeepers. Give them a piece of the cake without allowing them
to bite off more than they can chew. It's a rule which applies to all
training carried out by primary school children. The gradual development, if this policy is followed, should be straightforward. If a
boy is obviously an interested and promising 'keeper and has
clear personal qualities to develop, progress can be ambitious and
rapid.

Always encourage youngsters to look, listen and learn. One of
my early idols, Frank Swift, once wrote in his book, *Football in the
Goalmouth*: 'If you want to keep goal, fit yourself as well as you can
for the job,' and he followed this advice by seven points of the
greatest importance, humorously illustrated opposite.
1)   Keep your eye on the ball and your body behind it.
2)   Profit by your own mistakes. Hold an 'inquest' on all shots
which beat you.
3)   Reach an understanding with the whole of the team, not just
the defenders.

4)   Learn to call to your defence.
5)   Vary your goal kicks and clearances.
6)   Get it firmly fixed in your mind that when the ball is in the six-yard area it is yours.
7)   Watch and study top-line goalkeepers – I learned that way.

Frank Swift faithfully adhered to these points and they helped him become a truly great 'keeper for Manchester City and England. They will also go a long way towards helping the young schoolboy to learn the art of goalkeeping, because they are just as accurate and important now as they were in Frank's day.

10

It takes all sorts

I pondered for some time thinking of a suitable way to bring this book on goalkeeping to a close. Then while reading the text in its entirety I kept visualizing moments when I personally had experienced the problems that I was writing about or had seen some fellow 'keeper cope with the situation.

Time and again different techniques and methods flashed vividly across my mind. For instance, the way I faced an opponent who was clean through with the ball at his feet was entirely different from one of my contemporaries, Pat Jennings. Invariably Pat would stay upright until the very last second and then react to a shot, while yours truly would look for a moment of miscontrol and plunge head-first at the forward's feet. It was never a case of whose method was best. Pat's system worked perfectly for him and my kamikaze style suited me ideally. The success rate for both of us was high, and as long as the ball was consistently kept out of the net, that was the end of the argument.

Developing your own style I feel is the very key to goalkeeping. By all means hero-worship one of the current greats, but don't fall into the trap of trying to copy anyone's style totally. My 'style' was *similar* to Trautmann's but only similar. Bert was better at certain areas of goalkeeping than me, and I like to think there were a couple of aspects where I had the edge. It's really a matter of making a brutally honest early assessment of your ability and then polishing the natural diamond in your play. From then on, you have to work desperately hard at all the other aspects which are required. It's been this way with goalkeepers since football began and it's hardly likely to change now.

The greatest 'keeper of all time? Who knows? History only relates the names, dates and feats of many great men, but no one has ever been able to find a satisfactory way of proving the argument.

Many of the older generation still point to Sam Hardy as the greatest. Sam played between 1905 and 1920 and came from my birthplace, Chesterfield. His finest games were with Aston Villa and England and his greatest assets were his uncanny positioning and angling. The late Charles Buchan once recalled how in 1913 Hardy lost his mobility after suffering a leg injury but was still able to defy all the efforts of the Sunderland attack to help Aston Villa win the FA Cup 1-0. Sam Hardy also kept a clean sheet for Villa in the 1920 FA Cup final. He played nineteen times for England and eventually ended his playing career at Nottingham Forest before retiring to Chesterfield, where his career had begun.

I am told there were great similarities in style between Hardy and Harry Hibbs. Once again his secret was the art of anticipation. It is even claimed that Hibbs built up a library of information about players and would force them into corners they disliked. With raw recruits he would simply leave an obvious gap to one side and, to his great satisfaction, pounce on the ensuing shots.

Hibbs, like Hardy and Gordon Banks in later years, was able to make things look simple. Not for him a two-and-a-half somersault with twist! Instead he preferred where possible to make a quick adjustment with the feet and save without even diving. Harry Hibbs played twenty-five times for England and was often referred to as the 'second Sam Hardy'. High praise but inaccurate – the Birmingham 'keeper was really the 'first Harry Hibbs'. Incidentally Hibbs stood only 5 feet 9 inches tall, and although he evidently possessed tremendous spring and gymnastic ability, it proves yet again that in goalkeeping 'it takes all sorts'.

It is just possible that both Hibbs and Hardy would have frowned a little at the antics of another great 'keeper, Frank Swift, a man who was 6 feet 3 inches and who was known affectionately as Big Swifty. The Manchester City giant was the only goalkeeper ever to captain England and played in nineteen full and fourteen wartime internationals.

Sadly Frank was killed in the 1958 Munich air crash, when he was covering Manchester United's European Cup tie against Red Star Belgrade as a journalist. He will never be forgotten though, and neither will his goalkeeping, a mixture of brilliant play and showmanship. When asked once about the showy side of his game he replied: 'Oh well, I had to throw in a bit to please the crowd. Football is only a game after all.'

For a 'keeper who stood well over six feet tall, Swift was remarkably agile, and perhaps the greatest testimony to his ability is that outstanding 'keepers like Bert Williams of Wolves and Ted Ditchburn of Spurs had limited international experience because of the genial giant.

Apart from the early references in this chapter to Bert Trautmann and Pat Jennings, all the greats I've mentioned so far are English. Also deserving of a special mention in the roll of honour are Elisha Scott of Liverpool and Northern Ireland and Jack Kelsey of Arsenal and Wales, two men who were capable of that indefinable extra touch of greatness.

There have been numerous other fine British 'keepers through the years, but not too many from the Continent. For a long time the foreign 'keepers spoilt themselves by ignoring the British rule, 'simplicity and safety'. A more appropriate code for them would have been 'spectacular and sloppy'.

The worst of the showy Continentals was the pre-war Italian 'keeper, Olivieri. Journalist John Macadam wrote of him:

> Nothing was too easy for Olivieri to make look difficult. A simple pass back from one of his defenders and Olivieri tensed every muscle in his body, gathered himself like the clouds on Snowdon, coiled – and struck. He would leap in the air, flatten out, describe a graceful parabola and then sweep on the inoffensive ball with the venom of a stoat fastening on a rabbit. Then with a magnificent gesture he would bound to his feet, run to the edge of the penalty box and kick the ball out of sight – straight up in the air!

There is little doubt there is a certain degree of journalistic licence about this description, but it is true that Olivieri was possibly the biggest goalkeeping clown ever seen.

'Clown' is the choice of word Brian Clough once used to describe Poland's international 'keeper Jan Tomaszewski after his country had ended England's hopes of appearing in the 1974 World Cup finals. He was implying that Tomaszewski had made a series of lucky saves in the drawn game at Wembley which decided the group. Clough was unable to appreciate that the Pole's style of 'keeping was always like that. The fact is that the style suited him. Tomaszewski was a 'keeper who was prepared to gamble, take a chance and make his own luck. His brilliant performances in Poland's goal in both the 1974 and 1978 World Cup finals proved that he was no 'clown' but rather a 'keeper who had come to terms with certain deficiencies in technique and overcome them by developing a style of his own. Jan Tomaszewski was of my own era, but the best foreign 'keepers I saw as a youth were Beara of Yugoslavia, Grosics of Hungary and Yashin of Russia.

The last of these, Lev Yashin, often gave the impression of being an octopus. He always dressed himself completely in black and his long legs and elastic arms seemed to penetrate impossible zones. I will never forget one save he made when playing for a World XI against England and Wembley. It came shortly before half time and it was one of the most unorthodox saves I've ever seen; a forearm punch of a powerfully struck shot, which only came down to earth on the halfway line. There was a gasp from the 100,000 crowd, and the goalkeepers amongst them made a mental note of a 'new technique'.

Other foreign 'keepers I have admired for showing similar improvisations include Dino Zoff of Italy, Ladislav Mazurkiewicz of Uruguay, Ronnie Hellstroem of Sweden and Sepp Maier of West Germany.Maier in particular was a favourite of mine. He was a much maligned goalkeeper. Critics ridiculed his physique, his outrageous dress and jovial comic nature. But the records show that season after season Maier performed consistently well at international level and for his club side, Bayern Munich. He won every honour open to him, including a World Cup winner's medal, and he was without question a great, great goalkeeper.

Three of England's 'keepers of my time fall into the same category as Maier: Gordon Banks, Peter Shilton and Ray Clemence. Incidentally, that is not the order in which I would place them. They were all masters of their trade and each was clearly better than the other in one aspect or another. Banks was the master of positional play, Shilton the dominating character of the six-yard box, and Clemence the clear winner when it came to reading play and preventing trouble before it began.

Banks, Shilton, Clemence, Bonetti, Corrigan, Parkes, Stepney, Waiters, Springett, West, McDonald, Hodgkinson, Hopkinson,

Gregg, Finlayson, Brown, and of course the great Bert Trautmann. Just a random selection of goalkeepers whom I either played against or learned from. Throughout my career I never stopped looking and learning, absorbing and digesting every useful piece of information I could lay my hands on. I knew, however, that it was dangerous to attempt to become a carbon copy of any one individual, so the snippets of information that were gathered were only beneficial to my own particular style of goalkeeping.

How would I describe that style? Certainly not manufactured, which is a label one or two notable managers pinned upon me. As I see it all footballers fall into three categories.

There are those like Pele, Cruyff and George Best, who are born with an abundance of outstanding natural talent.

Others have a couple of real diamonds in a sound all-round game which ultimately puts them into international class.

And finally there are the less fortunate who work hard and enthusiastically to develop a solid but unspectacular performance.

Well, I was no Pele, but at the same time I was lucky to have a couple of very natural areas within my game – the ability to dive at an opponent's feet and a fiercely competitive, highly enthusiastic spirit. The two never failed me, and even when my punching or positional play left a lot to be desired, they sustained my goalkeeping credibility.

Mine wasn't an *elegant* style of goalkeeping, by any stretch of the imagination. I think *alert* was a good way of describing it. Perhaps even more accurate is a description I once read in *The Guardian* newspaper, one which brought home to me the importance of recognizing and sticking to one's natural style. What made the report so interesting to me was that it appeared exactly one week to the day after a remarkable report on one of my heroes, Pat Jennings, then with Spurs. Pat's style was totally opposite to mine. He really was elegant, and after a stunning game against Leeds United *The Guardian*'s reporter wrote an equally gracious account of the Irishman's performance:

> If Jennings had been available on that memorable day when the Romans met the Etruscans, Horatius surely would have had to have been satisfied with a seat on the substitutes' bench.

A classic account of a goalkeeper with classic style.

One week later the same newspaper reported Arsenal's game, which ironically was also against Leeds. In all modesty I have to admit that like Jennings I had a very good match, and when I realized the reporter was the same one who had praised Pat so highly seven days earlier, I was eager to read how I compared. This is what met my eyes:

> To play the way Wilson plays you need courage, speed of thought, determination . . . and an IQ of 20!

Upset? Not a bit of it. In its way the assessment of me appealed just as much as the one about Pat Jennings. The reporter had simply recognized two goalkeepers with two very distinct styles, one coolly calculating, the other calmly committed. Each method suited the individual perfectly. Each was effective.

That's the great thing about goalkeeping . . . . it takes all sorts.

Index